The Complete Book of Rhymes, Songs, Poems, Fingerplays, and Chants

Compiled by
Jackie Silberg and Pam Schiller

Dedication

To my mother, who read me Mother Goose before I was even born and continued to teach me the love of words throughout my life.

—Pam Schiller

To my parents Bertha and Sol Silberg who gave me "A Child's Garden of Verses" by Robert Louis Stevenson when I was sick with the chickenpox. The wonderful poetry sparked my interest in rhymes, chants, songs, and fingerplays.

—Jackie Silberg

Acknowledgments

To my editor Kathy Charner, who always has patience, kindness, wonderful ideas, and a great sense of humor.

To Larry and Leah Rood, owners of Gryphon House, who have always believed in my work and encouraged me through the years.

To Pam Schiller who has been a joy to work with and has made this book special.

—Jackie Silberg

The Complete Book of
Rhymes, Songs, Poems, Fingerplays and Chants

OVER 700 selections

Jackie Silberg
Pam Schiller

Illustrated by Deborah C. Wright

gryphon house®, inc.
Beltsville, MD 20704

Copyright

Copyright © 2002 Jackie Silberg and Pam Schiller
Published by Gryphon House, Inc.
10726 Tucker Street, Beltsville MD 20705
Visit us on the web at www.gryphonhouse.com

Illustrations: Deborah C. Wright
Cover: Illustrated by Joan Waites

Bulk purchase

Gryphon House books are available at special discount when purchased in bulk for special premiums and sales promotions as well as for fund-raising use. Special editions or book excerpts also can be created to specification. For details, contact the Director of Marketing at the address above.

Disclaimer

The publisher and the authors cannot be held responsible for injury, mishap, or damages incurred during the use of or because of the activities in this book. The authors recommend appropriate and reasonable supervision at all times based on the age and capability of each child.

Every effort has been made to locate copyright and permission information.

Library of Congress Cataloging-in-Publication Data

The complete book of rhymes, songs, poems, fingerplays, and chants / [compiled by] Jackie Silberg and Pam Schiller ; illustrated by Deborah Wright.
      p. cm.
    Includes index.
    ISBN 0-87659-267-1
      1. Children'spoetry, American. 2. Children's poetry, English. 3. Nursery rhymes. 4. Finger play. 5. Chants. I. Silberg, Jackie, 1934– II. Schiller, Pamela Byrne.

PSS586.3 .C66 2002
811.008'9282--dc21

2002020765

Table of Contents

Introduction

One of the greatest joys of working with and raising young children is the opportunity to revisit your own childhood. This book will take you on a wonderful journey down memory lane, while you share the love of language with a new generation. All it takes to unleash the power of rhymes, songs, poems, fingerplays, chants, and tongue twisters is to have fun with them. And while children are having fun, they will also learn:

- listening skills
- about order and sequence
- concepts, such as colors, shapes, and counting
- memory skills
- vocabulary
- imagination
- about humor
- coordination
- spatial awareness
- body awareness
- relaxation
- and so much more!

When the day seems long and dull, try singing a rousing chorus of "She'll Be Comin' 'Round the Mountain" to get things back on track. Sometimes, having fun can be as simple as saying, "There once was a queen whose face was green." Choose some of your childhood favorites to share. Children will enjoy listening to your much loved songs and rhymes, and will surely treasure the memories you share with them.

More Than Fun

Aside from being fun to do, singing songs, saying poems and rhymes, and doing fingerplays with children helps them develop early literacy skills. Long before children encounter formal reading instruction and are asked to hear the subtle differences between the letter sounds of "b" and "d," they should have many opportunities to play with and fall in love with rhythm, rhyme, repetition, and structural sequence. Songs, poems, rhymes, chants, tongue twisters, and fingerplays are the perfect vehicles for these experiences.

Because the size of a child's vocabulary and his or her ability to discriminate sounds are two of the greatest predictors of how easily he or she will learn to read, it only makes sense to take advantage of this opportunity to lay the foundation for future reading success.

How to Use This Book

To teach rhymes, chants, songs, fingerplays, and tongue twisters:

- Sing or say the words that you want to teach. Repeat them several times.
- Sing or say one line, leaving out one word. For example: "Twinkle, twinkle, little _____."
- If you are teaching a song, speak the words in the correct rhythm before you add the melody.
- Demonstrate appropriate actions as you say or sing the words.
- Talk about the words of the song or rhyme. For example, what do the words mean in the song "Yankee Doodle"? What is happening? Where did Yankee Doodle go? How did he get there? What did he do once he arrived? Encourage the children to think about what is happening; this will help them to remember the words.
- Use pictures to reinforce the words. For instance, the nursery rhyme "Little Boy Blue" talks about sheep and cows. Find pictures of these and hold them up while you say the words.
- Say the words loudly or softly, fast or slow, in a high or low voice depending on which is appropriate. Try using a different voice to reinforce the meaning of the words. For example, you could teach a rain and thunder poem in a low voice. Teach the song "The Eensy Weensy Spider" in a high, soft voice.

Read through the index of first lines; they will help you remember rhymes, song, fingerplays, poems, tongue twisters, and chants that you might have forgotten. The index of theme connections will help you find selections that relate to a theme or children's interests.

The selections in this book are sure to have children (and you) grinning from ear to ear. Remember, the most important thing is to be enthusiastic! If you use the rhymes and chants that you enjoy, children will enjoy them too.

1, 2, 3

1, 2, 3
Father caught a flea.
Put him in the teapot,
To drink a cup of tea.

Theme Connections

Counting
Fleas
Food
Humor
Numbers

2, 4, 6, 8

2, 4, 6, 8, meet me at the garden gate.
If I'm late do not wait, 2, 4, 6, 8.

Theme Connections

Counting
Numbers

A

After My Bath

After my bath I try, try, try
To rub with a towel till I'm dry, dry, dry.
Hands to dry, and fingers and toes,
And two wet legs and a shiny nose.
Just think how much less time it'd take,
If I were a dog and could shake, shake, shake!

Theme Connections

Dogs
Parts of the Body
Self-esteem

Aiken Drum

There was a man lived in the moon,
Lived in the moon, lived in the moon,
There was a man lived in the moon,
And his name was Aiken Drum.

Refrain:　　　And he played upon a ladle,
　　　　　　A ladle, a ladle,

And he played upon a ladle,
And his name was Aiken Drum.

And his hat was made of good cream cheese,
Of good cream cheese, of good cream cheese,
And his hat was made of good cream cheese,
And his name was Aiken Drum.

Refrain

And his coat was made of good roast beef,
Of good roast beef, of good roast beef,
And his coat was made of good roast beef,
And his name was Aiken Drum.

Refrain

And his buttons made of penny loaves,
Of penny loaves, of penny loaves,
And his buttons made of penny loaves,
And his name was Aiken Drum.

Refrain

And his breeches made of haggis bags,
Haggis bags, haggis bags,
And his breeches made of haggis bags,
And his name was Aiken Drum.

Refrain

Make up your own description of Aiken Drum such as "His
eyes were made of pizza," "His coat was made of bacon," or
"His mouth was a banana."

Theme Connections

Clothing
Food
Humor
Sun, Moon, Stars

Air

Look up, look down, look all around,
Look everywhere.
You couldn't live without me,
I'm even in your chair—
What is my name?
(air)

Theme Connections

Humor
Spatial Relationships

Alack, Alack

Alack, alack the clouds are so black,
And my coat is so flimsy and thin.
If we further ride on, the rain will come down,
And wet little Sam to the skin.

Theme Connections

Clothing
Colors
Weather

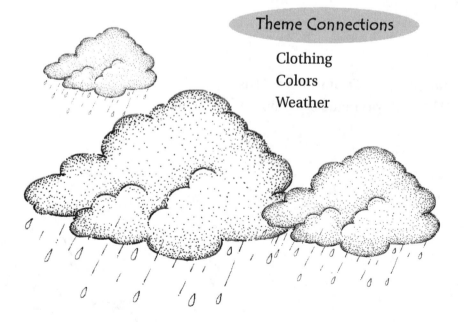

All About Me
by Jackie Silberg

All about me, I'm singing,
All about me 'cause I like me.
All about me, I'm singing,
All about me 'cause I like me.
I like my nose,
I like my toes,
And so I'll sing my song all day long.
I'm singing all about me,
I'm singing all about me,
I'm singing all about me 'cause I like me.

Theme Connections

Parts of the Body
Self-esteem

All by Myself

These are things I can do,
All by myself. *(point to self)*
I can comb my hair and fasten my shoe, *(point to hair and shoe)*
All by myself. *(point to self)*
I can wash my hands and wash my face, *(pretend to wash)*
All by myself. *(point to self)*
I can put my toys and blocks in place, *(pretend to put things away)*
All by myself. *(point to self)*

Theme Connections

Cleanup
Parts of the Body
Self-esteem

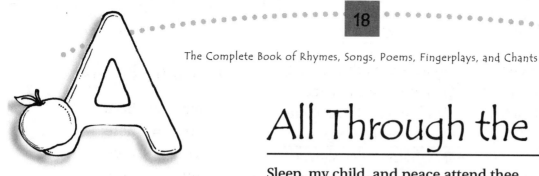

All Through the Night

Sleep, my child, and peace attend thee,
All through the night.
Guardian angels God will send thee,
All through the night.

Soft the drowsy hours are creeping,
Hill and vale in slumber sleeping,
I my loving vigil keeping,
All through the night.

While the moon her watch is keeping,
All through the night.
While the weary world is sleeping,
All through the night.

Theme Connections

Babies
Lullabies
Naptime/Sleeping
Sun, Moon, Stars

Alouette

Alouette, gentille Alouette,
Alouette je te plumerai.
Alouette, gentille Alouette,
Alouette je te plumerai.
Je te plumerai la tête,

Je te plumerai la tête,
Et la tête, et la tête,
Alouette, Alouette,
O-o-o-o-oh,
Alouette, gentille Alouette,
Alouette je te plumerai.

Alouette, gentille Alouette,
Alouette je te plumerai.
Alouette, gentille Alouette,
Alouette je te plumerai.
Je te plumerai la nez,
Je te plumerai la nez,
Et la tête, et la nez,
Alouette, Alouette,
O-o-o-o-oh,
Alouette, gentille Alouette,
Alouette je te plumerai.

Alouette, gentille Alouette,
Alouette je te plumerai.
Alouette, gentille Alouette,
Alouette je te plumerai.
Je te plumerai les yeux,
Je te plumerai les yeux,
Et la tête, et les yeux,
Alouette, Alouette,
O-o-o-o-oh,
Alouette, gentille Alouette,
Alouette je te plumerai.

Alouette, gentille Alouette,
Alouette je te plumerai.
Alouette, gentille Alouette,
Alouette je te plumerai.
Je te plumerai le cou,
Je te plumerai le cou,
Et la tête, et le cou,
Alouette, Alouette,
O-o-o-o-oh,
Alouette, gentille Alouette,
Alouette je te plumerai.

Alouette, gentille Alouette,
Alouette je te plumerai.
Alouette, gentille Alouette,
Alouette je te plumerai.
Je te plumerai les ailes,
Je te plumerai les ailes,
Et la tête, et les ailes,
Alouette, Alouette,
O-o-o-o-oh,
Alouette, gentille Alouette,
Alouette je te plumerai.

Alouette, gentille Alouette,
Alouette je te plumerai.
Alouette, gentille Alouette,
Alouette je te plumerai.
Je te plumerai le dos,
Je te plumerai le dos,
Et la tête, et le dos,
Alouette, Alouette,
O-o-o-o-oh,
Alouette, gentille Alouette,
Alouette je te plumerai.

English Translation

tête	=	head
nez	=	nose
yeux	=	eyes
cou	=	neck
ailes	=	wings
dos	=	back

Theme Connections

Languages
Parts of the Body

The Alphabet Forward and Backwards
(Tune: ABC Song)

A - B - C - D - E - F - G,
H - I - J - K - L - M - N - O - P,
Q - R - S,
T - U - V,
W - X,
Y and Z.
Now I know my ABCs.
Next time sing them backwards with me.

Z - Y - X - W - V - U - T
S - R - Q - P - O - N - M - L - K
J - I - H,
G - F - E,
D - C,
B and A
Now I've said my ZYXs.
Bet that's not what you expected!

Theme Connections

Alphabet
Humor

Alphabet Song

A - B - C - D - E - F - G
H - I - J - K - L - M - N - O - P
Q - R - S - T - U and V,
W - X - Y and Z.
Now I know my ABC's,
Next time won't you sing with me?

Variation

A, B, C, D, E, F, G,
H, I, J, K, L, M, N, O, P,
Q, R, S, T, U, and V,
W, X, Y, and Z.
Now I've said my ABC's;
Tell me what you think of me.

Theme Connections

Alphabet

America the Beautiful

Oh beautiful for spacious skies,
For amber waves of grain,
For purple mountain majesties
Above thy fruited plain.

America! America! God shed his grace on thee,
And crown thy good with brotherhood,
From sea to shining sea.

Oh beautiful for pilgrim feet,
Whose stern, impassioned stress,

A thoroughfare for freedom beat,
Across the wilderness.

America! America! God mend thine every flaw,
Confirm thy soul in self control,
Thy liberty in law.

Oh beautiful for patriot dreams,
That sees beyond the years;
Thine alabaster cities gleam,
Undimmed by human tears.

America! America! God shed his grace on thee,
And crown thy good with brotherhood,
From sea to shining sea.

Theme Connections

Colors
Holidays
Oceans and Seas
Patriotism

Anchors Aweigh

Anchors aweigh, my boys,
Anchors aweigh,
Farewell to college joys,
We sail at break of day.
Stand Navy out to sea,
Through swirling foam,
Until we meet once more,
Here's wishing you a happy voyage home.

Theme Connections

Boats and Ships
Houses and Homes
Oceans and Seas
Patriotism
Sailing

Animal Fair

I went to the animal fair,
The birds and the beasts were there.
The big baboon by the light of the moon,
Was combing his auburn hair.
You should have seen the monk!
He sat on the elephant's trunk.
The elephant sneezed and fell on her knees.
And what became of the monk?
The monk, the monk, the monk?

Theme Connections

| Colors | Humor | Sun, Moon, Stars |
| Elephants | Monkeys | |

Annie Mae

Annie Mae, where are you going?
Up the stairs to take a bath.
Annie Mae with legs like toothpicks
And a neck like a giraffe.
Annie Mae stepped in the bathtub.
Annie Mae pulled out the plug.
Oh my goodness!
Oh my soul!
There goes Annie Mae down that hole.
Annie Mae?
Annie Mae?
Gurgle, gurgle, glug.

Theme Connections

Giraffes
Humor

The Ants Go Marching

The ants go marching one by one,
Hurrah, hurrah.
The ants go marching one by one,
Hurrah, hurrah.
The ants go marching one by one,
The little one stops to suck his thumb.
And they all go marching down,
To the ground,
To get out,
Of the rain.
BOOM! BOOM! BOOM! BOOM!

…two…tie her shoe…
…three…climb a tree…
…four…shut the door…
…five…take a dive…
…six…pick up sticks…
…seven…pray to heaven…
…eight…shut the gate…
…nine…check the time…
…ten…say "The End!"

Theme Connections

Ants
Humor
Numbers
Sounds of Language
Weather

Apples and Bananas

I like to eat eat eat apples and bananas.
I like to eat eat eat apples and bananas.

I like to ate ate ate ay-ples and bay-nay-nays.
I like to ate ate ate ay-ples and bay-nay-nays.

I like eet eet eet ee-ples and bee-nee-nees.
I like eet eet eet ee-ples and bee-nee-nees.

I like to ite, ite, ite, i-ples and by-by-nys
I like to ite, ite, ite, i-ples and by-by-nys

I like to ote ote ote oh-ples and bo-no-nos.
I like to ote ote ote oh-ples and bo-no-nos.

I like to ute ute ute uupples and bununus.
I like to ute ute ute uupples and bununus.

Now we're through, through, through, through,
Now we're through with the apples and bananas,
Now we're through, through, through, through,
With A E I O and U.

Theme Connections

Alphabet
Apples
Food
Sounds of Language

April Clouds

Two little clouds one April day,
   (hold both hands in fists)
Went sailing across the sky.
   (move fists from left to right)
They went so fast that they bumped their heads,
   (bump fists together)
And both began to cry.
   (point to eyes)
The big round sun came out and said,
   (make circle with arms)
"Oh, never mind, my dears,
   I'll send all my sunbeams down
   (wiggle fingers downward like rain)
   To dry your fallen tears."

Theme Connections

Emotions
Months of the Year
Sun, Moon, Stars
Weather

Are You Sleeping?

Are you sleeping,
Are you sleeping,
Brother John, Brother John?
Morning bells are ringing,
Morning bells are ringing.
Ding! Dong! Ding!
Ding! Dong! Ding!

French Translation

Frere Jacques
Frere Jacques, Frere jacques
Dormez-vous? Dormez-vous?
Sonnez les matines, sonnez les matines
Din, din, don! Din, din, don!

¿Fray Felipe, Fray Felipe?
Fray Felipe, Fray Felipe
Duermes tú? Duermes tú?
Suenan las campanas.
Suenan las campanas.
Din, dan, don. Din, dan, don.

Theme Connections

Families
Languages
Sounds of Language
Time of Day

Arroró mi niño
(Hush Now, My Little One)

Arroró mi niño. Arroró mi sol.
Arroró pedazo de mi corazón.
Duermete mi niño. Duermete mi amor.
Duermete pedazo de mi corazón.
Arrurú mi niño que te canto yo.
Arrurú mi niño que ya se durmió.

English Translation

Hush now, my little one. Hush now, my sunshine.
Hush now, piece of my heart.
Go to sleep, my little one. Go to sleep, my love.
Go to sleep, piece of my heart.
Sleep, my little one, while I sing to you.
Sleep, my little one, who is already asleep.

Theme Connections

Emotions
Lullabies
Naptime/Sleeping

Arroz con leche
(Rice with Milk)

Arroz con leche; me quiero casar con una viudita de la capital,
que sepa coser, que sepa bordar,
que ponga la mesa en su santo lugar.
Yo soy la viudita, la hija del Rey.
me quiero casar y no hallo con quien.
contigo, sí. contigo, no.
contigo, mi amor, me casaré vo.

Rice with milk; I want to marry,
A sweet little widow from the capital city,
Who is able to sew, who is able to embroider,
And set a fine table.
I am the pretty little widow,
And the daughter of the king.
I wish to marry, but I don't know with whom.
With you, yes. With you, no.
With you my love, I will marry you.

Theme Connections

Emotions

As I Was Going to Banbury

As I was going to Banbury,
All on a summer's day,
My wife had butter, eggs, and cheese
And I had corn and hay.
Bob drove the kine* and Tom the swine.
Dick led the foal and mare.
I sold them all, then home again,
We came from Banbury fair.

Theme Connections

Farms
Food
Horses
Pigs
Seasons

* Kine is an old English word for cow.

As I Was Going to Sell My Butter

As I was going to sell my eggs,
Whom should I meet but Bandy legs.
Bandy legs and crooked toes,
Stir about cheeks and a teapot nose.
As I was going to sell my butter,
Whom should I meet but Stump in the Gutter.
Stump in the Gutter in a high-collared cap.
Upon my word it made me laff.

Theme Connections

Food
Humor

As I Was Going to St. Ives

As I was going to St. Ives,
I met a man with seven wives.
Each wife had seven sacks,
Each sack had seven cats,
Each cat had seven kits:
Kits, cats, sacks, and wives,
How many were going to St. Ives?

Theme Connections

Cats
Counting
Families
Numbers

Answer: One was going to St. Ives. Only one person was going to St. Ives. Another man +his seven wives + 49 sacks + 343 cats + 2401 kit(ten)s = 2801 coming from St. Ives.

As I Was Walking
(in a field of wheat)

As I was walking in a field of wheat,
I picked up something good to eat;
Neither fish, flesh, fowl, nor bone,
I kept it till it ran alone.
(an egg)

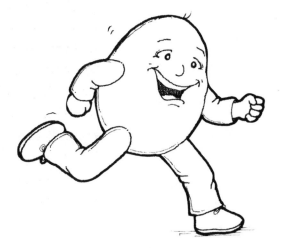

Theme Connections

Food
Humor

As I Was Walking
(near the lake)

As I was walking near the lake,
I met a little rattlesnake.
He ate so much of jelly-cake,
It made his little belly ache.

Theme Connections

Food
Humor
Snakes

As I Went to Bonner

As I went to Bonner,
I met a pig,
Without a wig,
Upon my word and honor.

Theme Connections

Humor
Pigs

As I Went Up the Apple Tree

As I went up the apple tree,
All the apples fell on me.
Bake a pudding, bake a pie,
Send it up to John MacKay.
If John MacKay is not in,
Send it up to the man in the moon.

Theme Connections

Apples
Cooking
Food
Sun, Moon, Stars

As Light as a Feather

As light as a feather,
As round as a ball,
Yet all the king's men,
Cannot carry it at all.
(a bubble)

Theme Connections

Humor
Kings and Queens

Au Clair de la Lune
(By the Light of the Moon)

Au clair de la lune,
Mon ami Pierrot,
Prete-moi ta plume
Pour ecrire un mot.
Ma chandelle est morte,
Je n'ai plus de feu;
Prete-moi ta plume
Pour l'amour de Dieu.

English Translation

By the light of the moon,
My good friend Pierrot,
Lend to me your pen,
So I may write a note.
See, my candle's guttered
Dim and chill my way;
Lend it to me,
For the love of God, I pray.

Theme Connections

Languages
Lullabies
Naptime/Sleeping
Sun, Moon, Stars

Aunt Maria

Aunt Maria, she sat on the fire.
The fire was too hot, she sat on the pot.
The pot was too round, she sat on the ground.
The ground was too flat, she sat on the cat.
The cat ran away with Maria on her back.

Theme Connections

Cats
Families
Humor

Auntie, Will Your Dog Bite?

Auntie, will your dog bite?
No, child, no!
Chicken in the bread tray,
Making up dough.

Auntie, will your oven bake?
Yes, just try!
What's that chicken good for?
Pie! Pie! Pie!

Auntie, is your pie good?
Good as you can expect!
Chicken in the bread tray,
Peck! Peck! Peck!

Theme Connections

Chickens
Cooking
Dogs
Families

Autumn Leaves

Autumn leaves are falling, falling, falling.
  (move from standing position to squatting)
Autumn leaves are spinning, spinning, spinning.
  (stand and turn)
Autumn leaves are floating, floating, floating.
  (sway side to side)
Autumn leaves are turning, turning, turning.
  (turn slowly)
Autumn leaves are dancing, dancing, dancing.
  (stand on toes, sway forward and back)
Autumn leaves are blowing, blowing, blowing.
  (take several steps forward)
Autumn leaves are falling, falling, falling.
  (squat)
Autumn leaves are sleeping, sleeping, sleeping.
  (place hands together on side of face)

Theme Connections

Nature
Seasons

Baby Bear's Chicken Pox
by Jackie Silberg

"Waa, waa, waa," cried baby bear.
"I've got chicken pox in my hair.
On my nose and everywhere.
Waa, waa, waa," cried baby bear.

"Oh poor baby," mommy said.
"Come to me and rest your head.
Soon you will be out of bed.
Oh poor baby," mommy said.

Theme Connections

Bears
Emotions
Humor
Parts of the body

Baby Bumblebee

I caught myself a baby bumblebee.
Won't my mommy be so proud of me?
I caught myself a baby bumblebee,
Ouch! He stung me!

I'm talking to my baby bumblebee.
Won't my mommy be so proud of me?
I'm talking to my baby bumblebee,
"Oh," he said, "I'm sorry."

I'm letting go my baby bumblebee.
Won't my mommy be so proud of me?
I'm letting go my baby bumblebee,
Look! He's happy to be free!

Theme Connections

Bees
Families

Baby Mice

Where are the baby mice?
Squeak, squeak, squeak. *(hide your hand behind your back)*
I cannot see them peek, peek, peek. *(bring your fist forward)*
Here they come out of their hole.
One, two, three, four, five, and that is all. *(open your fingers one at a time)*

Theme Connections

Animal Sounds   Mice
Counting   Numbers

Baby Seeds

In a milkweed cradle, snug and warm,
  (*close fingers into fist*)
Baby seeds are hiding safe from harm.
Open wide the cradle, hold it high,
  (*open hand and hold it up high*)
Come along wind, help them fly.
  (*wiggle fingers*)

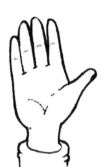

Theme Connections

Growing Things
Nature
Weather

The Baker

If a baker bakes for another baker,
Does the baker who bakes,
Bake the same way as the baker she is baking for?

Theme Connections

Cooking
Occupations
Sounds of Language

Barber, Barber

Barber, barber shave a pig.
How many hairs to make a wig?
Four and twenty, that's enough,
To give the barber a pinch of snuff.

Theme Connections

Numbers
Occupations
Pigs

Bat, Bat, Come Under My Hat

Bat, bat, come under my hat,
And I'll give you a slice of bacon.
And when I bake,
I'll give you a cake,
If I am not mistaken.

Theme Connections

Bats
Food

B-B-B-Baby
(Tune: K-K-K-Katy)

B-B-B-Baby, beautiful baby,
I love you more and more and more and more and more.
B-B-B-Baby, beautiful baby,
You're the only B-B-B-B-Baby that I adore!

Theme Connections

Babies
Emotions

Be Kind to Your Web-Footed Friends
(Tune: Stars and Stripes Forever)

Be kind to your web-footed friends,
For a duck may be somebody's mother.
Be kind to the birds in the swamp,
For the weather is very damp.
Oh, you may think that this is the end,
Well, it is!

Theme Connections

Birds
Ducks
Families
Weather

Be Very Quiet

Shhh! Be very quiet.
Shhh! Be very still.
Fold your busy little hands,
Close your sleepy little eyes.
Shhh! Be very quiet.

Theme Connections

Naptime/Sleeping
Parts of the Body

Bears Eat Honey

Bears eat honey.
Cows eat corn.
What do you eat
When you get up in the morn?
Monkeys eat bananas.
Cows eat corn.
What do you eat
When you get up in the morn?
Baby eats oatmeal,
Cows eat corn,
What do you eat
When you get up in the morn?

Theme Connections

Babies
Bears
Cows
Monkeys
Time of Day

The Bear

The other day,
(The other day)
I met a bear,
(I met a bear)
Away up there,
(Away up there)
A great big bear!
(A great big bear!)

The other day I met a bear,
A great big bear a way up there!

He looked at me,
(He looked at me)
I looked at him.
(I looked at him)
He sized up me,
(He sized up me)
I sized up him.
(I sized up him)

He looked at me, I looked at him.
He sized up me, I sized up him.

And so I ran,
(And so I ran)
Away from there.
(Away from there)
And right behind,
(And right behind)
Me was that bear.
(Me was that bear)

And so I ran away from there,
And right behind me was a that bear.

Ahead of me,
(Ahead of me)
I saw a tree,
(I saw a tree)
A great big tree,
(A great big tree)
Oh, golly gee!
(Oh, golly gee!)

Ahead of me there was a tree,
A great big tree, oh, golly gee!

The lowest branch,
(The lowest branch)
Was ten feet up.
(Was ten feet up)
I had to jump,
(I had to jump)
And trust my luck.
(And trust my luck)

The lowest branch was ten feet up,
I had to jump and trust my luck.

And so I jumped,
(And so I jumped)
Into the air,
(Into the air)
And missed that branch,
(And missed that branch)
Away up there.
(Away up there)

And so I jumped into the air,
And missed that branch away up there.

Now don't you fret.
(Now don't you fret)
And don't you frown.
(And don't you frown)
I caught that branch,
(I caught that branch)
On the way back down.
(On the way back down)

Now don't you fret and don't you frown,
I caught that branch on the way back down.

That's all there is.
(That's all there is)
There is no more.
(There is no more)
Until I meet,
(Until I meet)
That bear once more.
(That bear once more)

That's all there is, there is no more,
Until I meet that bear once more.

The end, the end.
(The end, the end)
The end, the end.
(The end, the end)
The end, the end.
(The end, the end)
The end, the end!
(The end, the end!)

The end, the end, the end, the end,
This time it really is the end!

Theme Connections

Bears
Nature

The Bear Went Over the Mountain

(Tune: For He's a Jolly Good Fellow)

The bear went over the mountain,
The bear went over the mountain,
The bear went over the mountain,
To see what he could see.

And all that he could see,
And all that he could see,
Was the other side of the mountain,
The other side of the mountain,
The other side of the mountain,
The other side of the mountain,
Was all that he could see.

Theme Connections

Bears
Senses

Bed Is Too Small

Bed is too small for my tiredness,
Give me a hilltop with trees.

Rock me to sleep in a cradle of dreams,
Send me a lullaby of leaves.

Theme Connections

Babies   Naptime/Sleeping
Lullabies   Nature

Bees

A swarm of bees in May,
Is worth a load of hay.
A swarm of bees in June,
Is worth a silver spoon.
A swarm of bees in July,
Isn't worth a fly.

Theme Connections

Bees
Months of the Year
Seasons

Betty Bought a Bit of Butter

Betty bought a bit of butter
But said she, "This butter's bitter.
If I put it in my batter
It will make my batter bitter."
So Betty bought a bit of better butter
And put it in her batter,
And it made her batter better.

Variation

Betty Botter bought some butter,
"But," she said, "The butter's bitter;
If I put it in my batter,
It will make my batter bitter;
But a bit of better butter,
That would make make my batter better."

Theme Connections

Cooking
Food
Sounds of Language

A Bicycle Built for Two

Daisy, Daisy, give me your answer true.
I'm half crazy all for the love of you.
It won't be a stylish marriage.
I can't afford a carriage.
But you'll look sweet, upon the seat
Of a bicycle built for two.

Theme Connections

Emotions
Families
Numbers

Big and Small

I can make myself real big, *(stand up on toes)*
By standing up straight and tall.
But when I'm tired of being big,
I can make myself get small. *(stoop down)*

Theme Connections

Growing Up
Opposites

The Big Bass Drum

Oh! We can play on the big bass drum,
And this is the way we do it:
Rub-a-dub, boom, goes the big bass drum,
And this is the way we do it.

Oh! We can play on the violin,
And this is the way we do it:
Zum, zum, zin, says the violin,
Rub-a-dub, boom goes the big bass drum,
And this is the way we do it.

Oh! We can play on the little flute,
And this is the way we do it:
Tootle, toot, toot, says the little flute,
Zum, zum, zin, goes the violin
Rub-a-dub, boom goes the big bass drum.
And this is the way we do it.

Theme Connections

Music
Sounds of Language

The Big Rock Candy Mountain

In the Big Rock Candy Mountains,
There's a land that's fair and bright.
Where the handouts grow on bushes,
And you sleep out ev'ry night.
Where the boxcars are all empty,
And the sun shines ev'ry day.
Oh, I'm bound to go where there ain't no snow,
Where the rain don't fall and the wind don't blow,
In the Big Rock Candy Mountains.

Oh, the buzzin' of the bees in the peppermint trees,
'Round the soda water fountains.
Where the lemonade springs and the bluebird sings,
In the Big Rock Candy Mountains.

In the Big Rock Candy Mountains,
You never change your socks.
And little streams of lemonade,
Come a-tricklin' down the rocks.
The hobos there are friendly
And their fires all burn bright.
There's a lake of stew and soda, too
You can paddle all around 'em in a big canoe
In the Big Rock Candy Mountains.

Oh, the buzzin' of the bees in the peppermint trees,
'Round the soda water fountains,
Where the lemonade springs and the bluebird sings,
In the Big Rock Candy Mountains.

Theme Connections

Bees
Food
Mountains
Trains
Weather

Big Ship Sailing

There's a big ship sailing on the illy ally oh,
Illy ally oh, illy ally oh.
There's a big ship sailing on the illy ally oh,
Hi, ho, illy ally oh.

There's a big ship sailing, rocking on the sea,
Rocking on the sea, rocking on the sea.
There's a big ship sailing, rocking on the sea,
Hi, ho, rocking on the sea.

There's a big ship sailing back again,
Back again, back again.
There's a big ship sailing back again,
Hi, ho, back again.

Variation

The big ship sails on the alley alley oh,
The alley, alley oh,
The alley, alley oh.
The big ship sails on the alley alley oh,
The last day of September.

Theme Connections

Boats and Ships
Oceans and Seas

Big Turkey

There was a big turkey on a steep green hill,
And he said, "Gobble, gobble, gobble, gobble."
His tail spread out like a big feather fan,
And he said, "Gobble, gobble, gobble, gobble."

Theme Connections

Animal Sounds
Holidays
Turkeys

Billy Boy

Oh, where have you been,
Billy Boy, Billy Boy?
Oh, where have you been,
Charming Billy?
I have been to seek a wife,
She's the joy of my life,
She's a young thing,
And cannot leave her mother.

Did she ask you to come in,
Billy Boy, Billy Boy?
Did she ask you to come in,
Charming Billy?
Yes, she asked me to come in,
There's a dimple in her chin.
She's a young thing,
And cannot leave her mother.

Can she make a cherry pie,
Billy Boy, Billy Boy?
Can she make a cherry pie,
Charming Billy?
She can make a cherry pie,
Quick as a cat can wink an eye.
She's a young thing,
And cannot leave her mother.

How old is she,
Billy Boy, Billy Boy?
How old is she,
Charming Billy?
Three times six and four times
seven,
Twenty-eight and eleven,
She's a young thing,
And cannot leave her mother.

Oh, where have you been,
Billy Boy, Billy Boy?
Oh, where have you been,
Charming Billy?
I have been to seek a wife,
She's the idol of my life.
She's a young thing,
And cannot leave her mother.

Where does she live,
Billy Boy, Billy Boy?
Oh, where does she live?
Charming Billy?
She lives on the hill,
Forty miles from the mill.
She's a young thing,
And cannot leave her mother.

Did she bid you to come in,
Billy Boy, Billy Boy?
Did she bid you to come in,
Charming Billy?
Yes, she bade me to come in,
And to kiss her on the chin.
She's a young thing,
And cannot leave her mother.

Did she take your hat,
Billy Boy, Billy Boy?
Did she take your hat,
Charming Billy?
Yes, she took my hat,
And she threw it at the cat.
She's a young thing,
And cannot leave her mother.

Did she set for you a chair,
Billy Boy, Billy Boy?
Did she set for you a chair,
Charming Billy?
Yes, she set for me a chair,
But the bottom wasn't there.
She's a young thing,
And cannot leave her mother.

Can she bake a cherry pie,
Billy Boy, Billy Boy?
Can she bake a cherry pie,
Charming Billy?
She can bake a cherry pie,
Quick as a cat can wink her eye.
She's a young thing,
And cannot leave her mother.

Can she make a feather bed,
Billy Boy, Billy Boy?
Can she make a feather bed,
Charming Billy?
She can make a feather bed,
That will rise above your head.
She's a young thing,
And cannot leave her mother.

Can she milk a heifer calf,
Billy Boy, Billy Boy?
Can she milk a heifer calf,
Charming Billy?
Yes, she can, and not miss
The bucket more than half.
She's a young thing,
And cannot leave her mother.

And is she very tall,
Billy Boy, Billy Boy?
And is she very tall,
Charming Billy?
She's as tall as any pine,
And as straight as a pumpkin
   vine.
She's a young thing,
And cannot leave her mother.

Are her eyes very bright,
Billy Boy, Billy Boy?
Are her eyes very bright,
Charming Billy?
Yes, her eyes are very bright,
But, alas, they're minus sight.
She's a young thing,
And cannot leave her mother.

Can she sing a pretty song,
Billy Boy, Billy Boy?
Can she sing a pretty song,
Charming Billy?
She can sing a pretty song,
But she often sings it wrong.
She's a young thing,
And cannot leave her mother.

How old may she be,
Billy Boy, Billy Boy?
How old may she be,
Charming Billy?
Three times six and four
   times seven,
Twenty eight and eleven,
She's a young thing,
And cannot leave her mother.

Theme Connections

Families
Food
Numbers

Bingo

There was a farmer had a dog,
And Bingo was his name-o.
B-I-N-G-O!
B-I-N-G-O!
B-I-N-G-O!
And Bingo was his name-o!

There was a farmer had a dog,
And Bingo was his name-o.
(Clap)-I-N-G-O!
(Clap)-I-N-G-O!
(Clap)-I-N-G-O!
And Bingo was his name-o!

There was a farmer had a dog,
And Bingo was his name-o.
(Clap, clap)-N-G-O!
(Clap, clap)-N-G-O!
(Clap, clap)-N-G-O!
And Bingo was his name-o!

There was a farmer had a dog,
And Bingo was his name-o.
(Clap, clap, clap)-G-O!
(Clap, clap, clap)-G-O!
(Clap, clap, clap)-G-O!
And Bingo was his name-o!

There was a farmer had a dog,
And Bingo was his name-o.
(Clap, clap, clap, clap)-O!
(Clap, clap, clap, clap)-O!
(Clap, clap, clap, clap)-O!
And Bingo was his name-o!

There was a farmer had a dog,
And Bingo was his name-o.
(Clap, clap, clap, clap, clap)
(Clap, clap, clap, clap, clap)
(Clap, clap, clap, clap, clap)
And Bingo was his name-o!

Spanish Translation

Había un perro en una granja
Y Bingo se llamaba.
B-I-N-G-O,
B-I-N-G-O,
B-I-N-G-O,
Y Bingo se llamaba.

Theme Connections

Dogs
Farms
Languages

Birds

If I were a bird, I'd sing a song,
And fly about the whole day long,
And when the night came,
Go to rest, up in my cozy little nest.

Theme Connections

Birds
Naptime/Sleeping
Time of Day

Birthday Candles

Birthday candles one-two-three.
   (hold up fingers on the count)
Birthday candles just for me!
   (point to self)
Last year two—next year four.
   (hold up two fingers on left hand and four fingers on right)
Birthday candles I want more!
   (hold up 10 fingers)

Theme Connections

Birthdays
Counting
Numbers

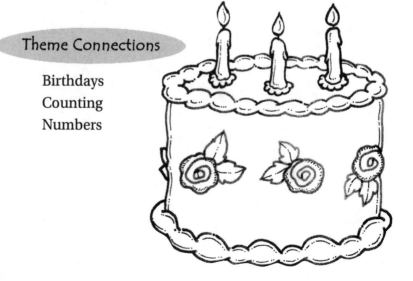

Blackberries

Blackberries, blackberries on the hill.
How many pails can you fill?
Briers are thick and briers scratch,
But we'll pick all the berries in the blackberry patch.

Theme Connections

Food
Work

Blow, Wind, Blow

Blow, wind, blow! And go, mill, go!
That the miller may grind his corn;
That the baker may take it,
And into bread make it,
And bring us a loaf in the morn.

Theme Connections

Food
Occupations
Weather

Bobby Shaftoe

Bobby Shaftoe went to sea,
Silver buckles on his knee.
He'll come back and marry me,
Pretty Bobby Shaftoe.
Bobby Shaftoe's fine and fair,
Combing down his auburn hair.
He's my friend for evermore,
Pretty Bobby Shaftoe.

Theme Connections

Colors
Emotions
Friends
Oceans and Seas

Boom, Boom, Ain't It Great to Be Crazy?

A horse and a flea and three blind mice,
Sat on a curbstone shooting dice.
The horse he slipped and fell on the flea.
"Whoops," said the flea, "There's a horse on me!"

Chorus:
Boom, boom, ain't it great to be crazy?
Boom, boom, ain't it great to be crazy?
Giddy and foolish the whole day through
Boom, boom, ain't it great to be crazy?

Way down south where bananas grow,
A flea stepped on an elephant's toe.
The elephant cried, with tears in his eyes,
"Why don't you pick on someone your own size?"

Chorus

Way up north where there's ice and snow
There lived a penguin and his name was Joe.
He got so tired of black and white,
He wore pink slacks to the dance last night!

Chorus

Eli, Eli had some socks
A dollar a pair and a nickel a box.
The more you wear 'em the better they get
And you put 'em in the water and they don't get wet!

Chorus

Called myself on the telephone
Just to hear that golden tone.
Asked myself out for a date
Said "Be ready 'bout half-past eight!"

Chorus

Theme Connections

Clothing	Mice
Elephants	Money
Fleas	Numbers
Horses	Penguins
Humor	Weather

Bounce the Ball
(Tune: Mulberry Bush)

This is the way we bounce the ball,
Bounce the ball, bounce the ball.
This is the way we bounce the ball,
Across the classroom floor.

Theme Connections

Movement
School

Bouncing Ball

I'm bouncing, bouncing, everywhere.
  (suit bouncing to words)
I bounce and bounce into the air.
I'm bouncing, bouncing like a ball.
I bounce and bounce until I fall.
  (drop to floor)

Theme Connections

Movement

"Bow Wow," Says the Dog

"Bow wow," says the dog.
"Meow meow," says the cat.
"Grunt, grunt," says the hog,
And "Squeak," says the rat.

"Tu-whu," says the owl.
"Caw, caw," says the crow.
"Quack, quack," goes the duck,
And "Moo," says the cow.

grunt!
grunt!

Theme Connections

Animal Sounds	Cows	Ducks
Cats	Dogs	Rats

Boys and Girls

Boys and girls come out to play,
The moon doth shine as bright as day.
Leave your supper and leave your sleep,
And join your playfellows in the street.
Come with a whoop and come with a call
Come with a good will or not at all.
Up the ladder and down the wall,
A tuppenny loaf will serve us all.
You bring milk and I'll bring flour,
And we'll have a pudding in half an hour.

Theme Connections

Cooking	Friends	Sun, Moon, Stars
Food	Money	

Brahm's Lullaby

Lullaby and good night, with roses bedight,
With lilies bedecked is baby's wee bed;
Lay thee down now and rest,
May thy slumber be blest.

Variation

Lullaby, and good night,
With pink roses bedight,
With lilies o'erspread,
Is my baby's sweet head.

Lay you down now, and rest,
May your slumber be blessed!
Lay you down now, and rest,
May thy slumber be blessed!

Lullaby, and good night,
You're your mother's delight,
Shining angels beside,
My darling abide.

Soft and warm is your bed,
Close your eyes and rest your head.
Soft and warm is your bed,
Close your eyes and rest your head.

Sleepyhead, close your eyes.
Mother's right here beside you.
I'll protect you from harm,
You will wake in my arms.

Lullaby, and sleep tight.
Hush! My darling is sleeping,
On his sheets white as cream,
With his head full of dreams.

When the sky's bright with dawn,
He will wake in the morning.
When noontide warms the world,
He will frolic in the sun.

Theme Connections

Babies
Lullabies
Naptime/Sleeping

Bryan O'Lynn

Bryan O'Lynn and his wife and wife's mother
They all went over a bridge together.
The bridge broke down and they all tumbled in.
"We'll go home by water," said Bryan O'Lynn.

Theme Connections

Families
Humor

Buenos Días
(Tune: Martinillo or Frey Felipe)

Buenos días, buenos días,
Cómo estás? ¿cómo estás?
Muy bien, gracias,
Muy bien, gracias,
Y usted? ¿y usted?

Buenas tardes, buenas tardes,
Cómo estás? ¿cómo estás?
Muy bien, gracias,
Muy bien, gracias,
Y usted? ¿y usted?

Buenas noches, buenas noches,
Cómo estás? ¿cómo estás?
Muy bien, gracias,
Muy bien, gracias,
Y usted? ¿y usted?

Sing days of the week in the same way.

Hoy es Lunes, hoy es Lunes,
cómo estás? ¿cómo estás?
Muy bien, gracias,
Muy bien, gracias,
Y usted? ¿y usted?
Martes
Miércoles
Jueves
Viernes
Sábado
Domingo

Buenos Días/Good Morning
(Tune: Are You Sleeping?)
Good morning, good morning,
How are you? How are you?
Very well, I thank you,
Very well I thank you,
How about you? How about you?

Good afternoon, good afternoon,
How are you? How are you?
Very well, I thank you,
Very well I thank you,
How about you? How about you?

Theme Connections

Days of the Week
Time of Day

Good evening, good evening,
How are you? How are you?
Very well, I thank you,
Very well I thank you,
How about you? How about you?

Sing days of the week in the same way.

Today is Monday, today is Monday,
How are you, how are you?
Very well, I thank you,
Very well I thank you,
How about you? How about you?

Tuesday
Wednesday
Thursday
Friday
Saturday
Sunday

Buffalo Gals

As I was walking down the street,
Down the street, down the street,
A pretty little gal I chanced to meet,
Oh, she was fair to see.

Chorus:
Buffalo Gals, won't you come out tonight,
Come out tonight, come out tonight.
Buffalo Gals, won't you come out tonight,
And dance by the light of the moon.

Theme Connections

Clothing
Humor
Movement
Parts of the Body
Sun, Moon, Stars

I stopped her and we had a talk,
Had a talk, had a talk,
Her feet took up the whole sidewalk,
And left no room for me.

Chorus

I asked her if she'd have a dance,
Have a dance, have a dance,
I thought that I might have a chance,
To shake a foot with her.

Chorus

I danced with a gal with a hole in her stockin',
And her heel kept a-knockin', and her toes kept a-rockin'.
I danced with a gal with a hole in her stockin',
And we danced by the light of the moon.

Chorus

Bumblebee

Bumblebee was in the barn,
  (circle finger in the air)
Carrying dinner under his arm.
  (move finger close to arm)
Buzzzzzzz-zz-z!
  (poke arm)

Theme Connections

Bees
Farms

The Bus

There is a painted bus,
With twenty painted seats.
It carries painted people
Along the painted streets.
They pull the painted bell,
The painted driver stops,
And they all get out together
At the little painted shops.

Theme Connections

Neighborhoods
Numbers
Transportation

Buttercups and Daisies

Buttercups and daisies,
Oh what pretty flowers,
Coming in the springtime,
To tell of sunny hours!
While the trees are leafless,
While the fields are bare,
Buttercups and daisies,
Spring up everywhere.

Theme Connections

Flowers
Seasons

Buying a Horse

One white foot, buy him.
Two white feet, try him.
Three white feet, look well about him.
Four white feet, do without him.

Theme Connections

Colors
Counting
Horses
Numbers

Bye Baby Bunting

Bye baby bunting, your daddy's gone a-hunting,
For to catch a rabbit skin, to wrap the baby bunting in.

Bye baby bunting, your mammy's gone the other way,
To beg a bowl of sour whey, for little baby bunting.

Variation

Bye, baby bunting
Father's gone a hunting,
Mother's gone a milking,
Sister's gone a silking,
Brother's gone to buy a skin,
To wrap the baby bunting in.

Theme Connections

Babies
Families

Cackle, Cackle Mother Goose

Cackle, cackle mother goose,
Have you any feathers loose?
Truly have I, pretty fellow,
Quite enough to fill a pillow.

Theme Connections

Geese

Calliope Song

(Divide children into four groups to make a human carousel. Group One says, "Oom-pah-pah," as they bend and then straighten their knees. Group Two says "oomp-tweedle-dee-dee," as they raise up on their tip-toes and back down. Group Three says, "Oom-Shh-Shh," as they rock back and forth. Group Four hums as they sway side to side.

Theme Connections

Music
Sounds

Can You Wash Your Father's Shirt?

Can you wash your father's shirt,
Can you wash it clean?
Can you wash your father's shirt,
And bleach it on the green?
Yes, I can wash my father's shirt,
And I can wash it clean.
I can wash my father's shirt,
And send it to the Queen.

Theme Connections

Clothing
Families
Kings and Queens
Opposites
Work

Cap, Mittens, Shoes, and Socks
(Tune: Head, Shoulders, Knees, and Toes)

Cap, mittens, shoes, and socks,
Shoes and socks.
Cap, mittens, shoes, and socks,
Shoes and socks.
And pants and belt, and shirt and tie,
Go together wet or dry,
Wet or dry!

Theme Connections

Clothing
Seasons

The Cat

The cat sat asleep by the side of the fire.
The mistress snored loud as a pig.
Jack took up his fiddle by Jenny's desire,
And struck up a bit of a jig.

Theme Connections

Cat
Music
Naptime/Sleeping

Catalina Magnalina

She had a peculiar name but she wasn't to blame.
She got it from her mother, who's the same, same, same.

Chorus
Catalina Magnalina, Hootensteiner Bogentwiner
Hogan Logan Bogan was her name.

She had two peculiar teeth in her mouth,
One pointed north and the other pointed south.

Chorus

She had two peculiar eyes in her head,
One was purple and the other was red.

Theme Connections

Colors
Humor
Opposites

Catch Him, Crow

Catch him, crow! Carry him, kite!
Take him away til the apples are ripe;
When they are ripe and ready to fall,
Here comes baby, apples and all.

Theme Connections

Apples
Babies
Birds
Seasons

The Complete Book of Rhymes, Songs, Poems, Fingerplays, and Chants

A Caterpillar Crawled

A caterpillar crawled,
  (*creep fingers up one arm*)
      To the top of the tree.
        "I think I'll take a nap," says he.
          (*place one hand over opposite fist*)
        So under a leaf he began to creep
      To spin his cocoon,
    And he fell asleep.

All winter long he slept in his bed,
'Til spring came along one day and said,
"Wake up, wake up, little sleepyhead,
  (*shake fist with other hand*)
Wake up, it's time to get out of bed."
So he opened his eyes that sunshiny day.
  (*spread fingers, hook thumbs*)
Lo! He was a butterfly, and flew away.
  (*flap hands as wings and fly away*)

Theme Connections

Butterflies
Caterpillars
Naptime/Sleeping
Seasons

Caterpillar

Who's that ticklin' my back? said the wall,
  (*crawl fingers up am*)
"Me," said a small caterpillar, "I'm learning to crawl."

Theme Connections

Caterpillars

Charlie Over the Ocean

Charlie over the ocean,
Charlie over the sea,
Charlie caught a blackbird,
But he can't catch me.

Theme Connections

Birds
Oceans and Seas

Chickery, Chickery, Cranny Crow

Chickery, chickery, cranny crow
Went to the well to wash my toe;
When I got back, my chicken was gone.
What'll I do from dusk to dawn?

Theme Connections

Chickens
Parts of the Body

Chocolate Rhyme

One, two, three, cho— *(count with fingers)*
One, two, three, co—
One, two, three, la—
One, two, three, te!
Stir, stir the chocolate. *(make stirring motion)*

Spanish Translation

Rima de chocolate
Uno, dos, tres, cho—
Uno, dos, tres, co—
Uno, dos, tres, la—
Uno, dos, tres, te!
Bate, bate, chocolate.

Theme Connections

Counting
Food
Numbers

Choosing a Kitten

A black-nosed kitten will slumber all the day;
A white-nosed kitten is ever glad to play;
A yellow-nosed kitten will answer to your call;
And a gray-nosed kitten I like best of all.

Theme Connections

    Cats
    Colors

Christmas Is Coming

Christmas is coming,
The geese are getting fat.
Please to put a penny in an old man's hat.
If you haven't got a penny, a ha'penny will do.
If you haven't got a ha'penny, God bless you.

Theme Connections

    Geese
    Holidays
    Money

Clap Your Hands

Clap your hands 1-2-3. *(suit movements to words)*
Clap your hands just like me.

Wiggle your fingers 1-2-3.
Wiggle your fingers just like me.

Theme Connections

Counting
Movement
Parts of the Body

Clementine

In a cavern, in a canyon,
Excavating for a mine,
Lived a miner forty-niner,
And his daughter, Clementine.

Chorus:
Oh, my darling, oh, my darling,
Oh, my darling Clementine,
You are lost and gone forever,
Dreadful sorry, Clementine.

Light she was and like a fairy,
And her shoes were number nine,
Herring boxes without topses,
Sandals were for Clementine.

Chorus

MINE

Drove her ducklings to the water,
Every morning just at nine.
Hit her foot against a splinter,
Fell into the foaming brine.

Chorus

Ruby lips above the water,
Blowing bubbles soft and fine,
But alas, I was no swimmer,
So I lost my Clementine.

Chorus

Theme Connections

Emotions
Families

The Clock

"Tick-tock, tick-tock,
Tick-tock" says the clock.
Little boy, little girl,
Time to wash our hands.

Theme Connections

Time of Day

Cloud

What's fluffy white and floats up high,
　　(point skyward)
Like a pile of cotton in the sky?
And when the wind blows hard and strong,
　　(wiggle fingers moving horizontally)
What very gently floats along?
　　(wiggle fingers moving downward)
What brings the rain?
　　　　(open hands palm up)
What brings the snow
　　That showers down on us below?
　　When you look up in the high blue sky,
　　(look up)
　　What is that thing you see float by?
　　(A cloud)

Theme Connections

Colors
Weather

Clouds

White sheep, white sheep,
On a blue hill,
When the wind stops,
You all stand still.
When the wind blows,
You walk away slow.
White sheep, white sheep.

Theme Connections

Colors
Sheep
Weather

Cobbler, Cobbler

Cobbler, cobbler, mend my shoe.
Get it done by half past two.
My little toe is peeping through.
Cobbler, cobbler, mend my shoe.
Get it done by half past two.

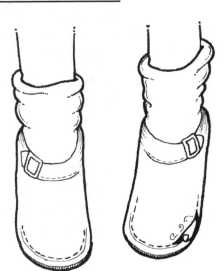

Theme Connections

Clothing
Occupations
Time of Day

Cock-a-Doodle-Doo

Cock-a-doodle-doo,
My dame has lost her shoe!
My master's lost his fiddling stick,
And doesn't know what to do,
And doesn't know what to do,
And doesn't know what to do,
My master's lost his fiddling stick,
And doesn't know what to do.

Theme Connections

Families
Roosters

Cockles and Mussels

In Dublin's fair city
Where girls are so pretty,
'Twas there I first met with
Sweet Molly Malone.

She drove a wheelbarrow,
Through streets broad and narrow.
Crying, "Cockles and mussels,
Alive, alive-o."

Chorus:
Alive, alive-o
Alive, alive-o
Crying, "Cockles and mussels,
Alive, alive-o."

She was a fishmonger,
But sure 'twas no wonder,
For so were her mother,
And father before.

They drove their wheelbarrows,
Through streets broad and narrow,
Crying, "Cockles and mussels,
Alive, alive-o."

Chorus

Theme Connections

Families
Food
Oceans and Seas
Work

The Cock's on the Housetop

The cock's on the housetop,
Blowing his horn.
The bull's in the barn,
A threshing the corn.
The maids in the meadow
Are making the hay.
The ducks in the river
Are swimming away.

Theme Connections

Bulls
Ducks
Farms
Rivers
Roosters

Color Song

Red is the color for an apple to eat.
Red is the color for cherries, too.
Red is the color for strawberries.
I like red, don't you?

Blue is the color for the big blue sky.
Blue is the color for baby things, too.
Blue is the color of my sister's eyes.
I like blue, don't you?

Yellow is the color for the great big sun.
Yellow is the color for lemonade, too.
Yellow is the color of a baby chick.
I like yellow, don't you?

Green is the color for the leaves on the trees.
Green is the color for green peas, too.
Green is the color of a watermelon.
I like green, don't you?

Orange is the color for oranges.
Orange is the color for carrots, too.
Orange is the color of a jack-o-lantern.
I like orange, don't you?

Purple is the color for a bunch of grapes.
Purple is the color for grape juice, too.
Purple is the color for a violet.
I like purple, don't you?

Theme Connections

Colors   Nature
Food   Sun, Moon, Stars

Come and Listen
(Tune: Are You Sleeping?)

Come and listen,
Come and listen,
To my song,
To my song.
Happy children singing,
Happy children singing,
Sing along, Sing along.

Theme Connections

Emotions
Music

Come, Butter, Come

Come, butter, come*.
Come, butter, come.
(Child's name)'s at the garden gate,
Waiting with banana cake.
Come, butter, come.

* Use this chant as children shake heavy cream into butter.

Theme Connections

Food

Counting

One for sorrow,
Two for joy,
Three for a kiss and four for a boy.
Five for silver,
Six for gold,
Seven for a secret never to be told.
Eight for a letter from over the sea.
Nine for my baby as sweet as can be.

Theme Connections

Counting
Numbers

The Cow
by Robert Louis Stevenson

The friendly cow all red and white,
I love with all my heart:
She gives me cream with all her might,
To eat with apple-tart.

She wanders lowing here and there,
And yet she cannot stray,
All in the pleasant open air,
The pleasant light of day;

Theme Connections

Cows
Colors
Emotions
Farms

And blown by all the winds that pass
And wet with all the showers,
She walks among the meadow grass
And eats the meadow flowers.

Crocodile Song

She sailed away on a bright and sunny day,
On the back of a crocodile.
"You see," said she, "he's as tame as he can be;
I'll ride him down the Nile."
The croc winked his eye as she bade her mom good-bye,
Wearing a happy smile.
At the end of the ride the lady was inside,
And the smile was on the crocodile!

Theme Connections

Crocodiles
Humor
Rivers

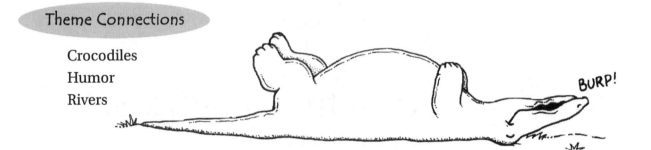

Crocodile

If you should meet a crocodile,
Don't take a stick and poke him.
Ignore the welcome of his smile,
Be careful not to stroke him,
For as he sleeps upon the Nile,
He gets thinner and thinner.
And whene'er you meet a crocodile,
He's looking for his dinner.

Theme Connections

Crocodiles

Cross Patch

Cross patch, draw the latch,
Sit by the fire and spin.
Take a cup and drink it up,
And let your neighbors in.

Theme Connections

Friends
Houses and Homes

¿Cuántos cuentos?
How many tales?

Cuando cuentes cuentos,
Cuenta cuántos cuentas,
Porque cuando cuentas cuentos,
Nunca sabes cuántos cuentos cuentas.

English Translation

When you tell tales,
How many tales do you tell?
Because when you tell tales,
You never know how many tales you tell.

Theme Connections

Humor

Curly Locks

Curly locks, curly locks,
Will you be mine?
You shall not wash dishes,
Nor feed the swine,
But sit on a cushion,
And sew a fine seam,
And feed upon strawberries,
Sugar, and cream.

Theme Connections

Emotions
Food
Work

Cushy Cow Bonnie

Cushy cow, Bonnie, let down thy milk,
And I will give thee a gown of silk.
A gown of silk and a silver tee,
If thou wilt let down thy milk for me.

Theme Connections

Cows
Farms
Food

D

Daffy Down Dilly

Daffy Down Dilly
Has come to town,
In a yellow petticoat,
And a green gown.

Theme Connections

Colors

Dance a Merry Jig

This little pig danced a merry, merry jig.
(touch toes or fingers as you say the words)
  This little pig ate candy.
  This little pig wore a blue and yellow wig.
  This little pig was a dandy.
  But this little pig never grew very big,
  And they called her itty bitty Mandy.

Theme Connections

Colors　　　Pigs

Dance, Thumbkin, Dance

Dance, Thumbkin, dance. *(dance thumbs around, moving
and bending them)*
Dance, ye merrymen, everyone. *(dance all fingers)*
For Thumbkin, he can dance alone,
Thumbkin, he can dance alone.

Dance, Foreman, dance. *(dance index fingers around,
moving and bending them)*
Dance, ye merrymen, everyone. *(dance all fingers)*
For Foreman, he can dance alone,
Foreman, he can dance alone.

Dance, Longman, dance. *(dance middle fingers around,
moving and bending them)*
Dance, ye merrymen, everyone. *(dance all fingers)*
For Longman, he can dance alone,
Longman, he can dance alone.

Dance, Ringman, dance. *(dance ring fingers around—they
won't bend alone)*
Dance, ye merrymen, everyone. *(dance all fingers)*
For Ringman, he cannot dance alone,
Ringman, he cannot dance alone.

Dance, Littleman, dance. *(dance little fingers around,
moving and bending them)*
Dance, ye merrymen, everyone. *(dance all fingers)*
For Littleman, he can dance alone,
Littleman, he can dance alone.

Theme Connections

Movement
Parts of the Body

De Colores

De colores, de colores,
Se visten los campos,
Enla primavera;
De colores, de colores,
Son los pajarillos,
Que vienen de afuera;
De colores, de colores,
Es el arco iris,
Que vemos lucir,
Y por eso,
Los grandes amores,
De muchos colores,
Me gustan a mí.

Variation

De colores,
De colores,
Bright with colors the mountains and valleys,
Dress up in the springtime,
De colores,
Bright with colors, all the little birds fill the skies in the day-
time.
De colores,
Bright with colors the rainbow brings joy with the glory of
spring.

Chorus:
And a bright love with colors has found us,
With peace all around us,
That makes our hearts sing.

Here the rooster singing kiri, kiri, kiri, kiri, kiri,
In the morning,
In the morning the hen sings her cara, cara, cara, cara,
All day singing,
Baby chicks all day sing pio, pio, pio, pio, pi.

Chorus

Theme Connections

Colors
Languages
Seasons

Deedle, Deedle, Dumpling

Deedle, deedle, dumpling, my son John,
Went to bed with his breeches on.
One shoe off and one shoe on,
Deedle, deedle, dumpling, my son John.

Theme Connections

Clothing
Families
Naptime/Sleeping

A Devonshire Rhyme

Walk fast in snow,
In frost walk slow,
And still as you go,
Tread on your toe.
When frost and snow are both together,
Sit by the fire and spare shoe leather.

Theme Connections

Opposites
Weather

Dickery, Dickery, Dare

Dickery, dickery, dare,
The pig flew up in the air.
The man in brown,
Soon brought him down!
Dickery, dickery, dare.

Theme Connections

Humor
Opposites
Pigs

Did You Ever See a Lassie?

Did you ever see a lassie, a lassie, a lassie?
Did you ever see a lassie go this way and that?
Go this way and that way, and this way and that way?
Did you ever see a lassie, go this way and that?

Theme Connections

Movement

Did You Feed My Cow?

Did you feed my cow?
Yes, ma'am!
Will you tell me how?
Yes, ma'am!
What did you feed her?
Corn and hay.
What did you feed her?
Corn and hay.

Did you milk her good?
Yes, ma'am!
Did you milk her like you should?
Yes, ma'am!
How did you milk her?
Swish, swish, swish!
How did you milk her?
Swish, swish, swish.

Theme Connections

Cows
Farms
Work

A Diller, A Dollar

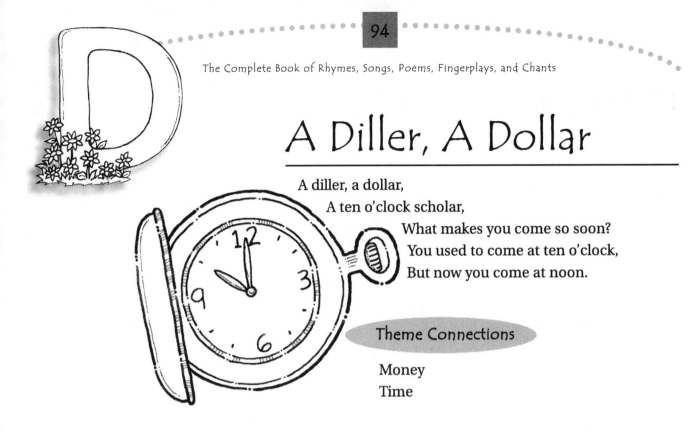

A diller, a dollar,
A ten o'clock scholar,
What makes you come so soon?
You used to come at ten o'clock,
But now you come at noon.

Theme Connections

Money
Time

Ding, Dong, Bell

Ding, dong, bell,
Pussy's in the well.
Who put her in?
Little Johnny Green.
Who pulled her out?
Little Tommy Stout.
What a naughty boy was that,
To try and drown old putty cat,
Who never did any harm,
But killed the mice in her father's barn.

Theme Connections

Cats
Emotions
Mice
Sounds of Language

Dinosaurs

Five enormous dinosaurs,
Letting out a roar—
One went away, and
Then there were four.

Four enormous dinosaurs,
Crashing down a tree—
One went away, and,
Then there were three.

Three enormous dinosaurs,
Eating tiger stew—
One went away, and,
Then there were two.

Two enormous dinosaurs,
Trying to run—
One ran away, and,
Then there was one.

One enormous dinosaur,
Afraid to be a hero—
He went away, and
Then there was zero.

Theme Connections

Counting
Dinosaurs

Dirty Old Bill

I know a man named Dirty Old Bill
He lives on top of a garbage hill.
Oh, he never took a bath and he never will.
Peeuuw! Dirty Old Bill!

Theme Connections

Humor
Senses

Do Your Ears Hang Low?

Do your ears hang low?
Do they wobble to and fro?
Can you tie them in a knot?
Can you tie them in a bow?
Can you throw them o'er your shoulder,
Like a Continental Soldier?
Do your ears hang low?

Do your ears hang high?
Do they reach up to the sky?
Do they wrinkle when they're wet?
Do they straighten when they're dry?
Can you wave them at your neighbor,
With an element of flavor?
Do your ears hang high?

Do your ears hang wide?
Do they flap from side to side?
Do they wave in the breeze,
From the slightest little sneeze?
Can you soar above the nation,

With a feeling of elevation?
Do your ears hang wide?

Do your ears fall off,
When you give a great big cough?
Do they lie there on the ground,
Or bounce up at every sound?
Can you stick them in your pocket,
Just like Davy Crocket?
Do your ears fall off?

Does your tongue hang down?
Does it flop all around?
Can you tie it in a knot?
Can you tie it in a bow?
Can you throw it o'er your shoulder,
Like a Continental Soldier?
Does your tongue hang down?

Does your nose hang low?
Does it wiggle to and fro?
Can you tie it in a knot?
Can you tie it in a bow?
Can you throw it o'er your shoulder,
Like a Continental Soldier?
Does your nose hang low?

Do your eyes pop out?
Do they bounce all about?
Can you tie them in a knot?
Can you tie them in a bow?
Can you throw them o'er your shoulder,
Like a Continental Soldier?
Do your eyes pop out?

Theme Connections

Humor
Parts of the Body

Donkey, Donkey

Donkey, donkey, old and gray,
Open your mouth and gently bray.
Lift your ears and blow your horn,
To wake the world this sleepy morn.
Donkey, donkey, do not bray,
But mend your pace and trot away.
Indeed, the market's almost done,
My butter's melting in the sun.
Gee up, Neddy, to the fair.
What shall I buy when I get there?
A ha'penny apple, a penny pear,
Gee up Neddy to the fair.

Theme Connections

Donkeys
Food
Money

The Donut Song
(Tune: Turkey in the Straw)

Oh, I ran around the corner,
And I ran around the block
I ran right in to the baker shop.
I grabbed me a donut,
Right out of the grease,
And I handed the lady,
A five-cent piece.
She looked at the nickel,
And she looked at me.
She said, "This nickel,
Ain't no good to me.
There's a hole in the nickel,
And it goes right through."
Said I, "There's a hole in your donut, too!
Thanks for the donut. Good-bye!"

Theme Connections

Food
Humor
Money

Neighborhoods
Occupations

Doodlebug

Doodlebug, doodlebug, come get sweet milk.
Doodlebug, doodlebug, come get some butter.
Doodlebug, doodlebug, come get corn bread.
Doodlebug, doodlebug, come get supper.

Theme Connections

Food

Doodle-li-do

Please sing to me that sweet melody,
Called Doodle-li-do, Doodle-li-do.
I like the rest, but the one I like best,
Goes Doodle-li-do, Doodle-li-do.
It's the simplest thing, there isn't much to it.
All you gotta do is Doodle-li-do it.
I like it so that wherever I go,
It's the Doodle-li, Doodle-li-do.

Come on and Waddle-li-atcha, Waddle-li-atcha,
Waddle-li-o, Waddle-li-o.
Waddle-li-atcha, Waddle-li-atcha
Waddle-li-o, Waddle-li-o.

It's the simplest thing, there isn't much to it.
All you gotta do is Doodle-li-do it.
I like it so that wherever I go,
It's the Doodle-li-Doodle-li-do.

*Perform these movements in rhythm with the music. Clap
thighs twice. Clap hands twice. Cross hands in front of you
four times (left hand on top twice, then right hand on top
twice). Touch nose then right shoulder with left hand. Touch
nose then left shoulder with right hand. Move hands in
"talking" motion just above shoulders, then above head.
Repeat throughout the song.*

Theme Connections

Movement
Music
Sounds of Language

Dormy, Dormy Dormouse

Dormy, dormy, dormouse,
Sleeps in his little house.
He won't wake up 'til suppertime,
And that won't be 'til half past nine.

Theme Connections

> Mice
> Naptime/Sleeping
> Time of Day

Down by the Bay

Down by the bay where the watermelons grow.
Back to my home I dare not go.
For if I do my mother will say,
"Did you ever see a pig dancing the jig?"
Down by the bay.

Additional verses:
…"Did you ever see a whale with a polka dot tail?"…
…"Did you ever see a bear combing his hair?"…
…"Did you ever see a moose kissing a goose?"…
…"Did you ever see a bee with a sunburned knee?"…

Theme Connections

> Bees
> Humor
> Moose
> Pigs
> Seasons
> Whales

Down by the Riverside

I'm gonna lay down my heavy load,
Down by the riverside,
Down by the riverside,
Down by the riverside,
I'm gonna lay down my heavy load,
Down by the riverside.

I ain't gonna study war no more
Down by the riverside,
Down by the riverside,
Down by the riverside.
I ain't gonna study war no more,
    Down by the riverside.

    I'm gonna lay down my sword and shield,
  Down by the riverside,
    Down by the riverside,
     Down by the riverside.
     I'm gonna lay down my sword and
     shield,
    Down by the riverside.

I'm gonna lay down my travelin' shoes,
Down by the riverside,
Down by the riverside,
Down by the riverside.
I'm gonna lay down my travelin' shoes,
Down by the riverside.

I'm gonna put on my long white robe,
Down by the riverside,
Down by the riverside,
Down by the riverside.
I'm gonna put on my long white robe,
Down by the riverside.

I'm gonna put on my starry crown,
Down by the riverside,
Down by the riverside,
Down by the riverside.
I'm gonna put on my starry crown,
Down by the riverside.

Theme Connections

Peace
Rivers

Down by the Station

Down by the station,
Early in the morning,
See the little puffer-bellies,
All in a row.

See the engine driver,
Pull the little throttle.
Puff, puff! Toot, toot!
Off we go.

Theme Connections

Sounds of Language
Time of Day
Trains

Downy Duck

One day I saw a downy duck
With feathers on his back.
I said, "Good morning, downy duck."
And he said, "Quack, quack, quack."

Theme Connections

Animal Sounds
Ducks
Time of Day

Dr. Foster Went to Gloucester

Dr. Foster went to Gloucester
In a shower of rain.
He stepped in a puddle
Right up to his middle
And never went there again.

Theme Connections

Occupations
Weather

Dusty
(Tune: Bingo)

There was a cowboy,
Rode a horse,
And Dusty was his name-o.
D-U-S-T-Y
D-U-S-T-Y
D-U-S-T-Y
And Dusty was his name-o.

Theme Connections

Cowboys/Cowgirls
Horses

E

Eeny, Meeny, Miney, Mo

Eeny, meeny, miney mo.
Catch a tiger by the toe.
If he hollers, let him go.
Eeny, meeny, miney mo.

Theme Connections

Humor
Tigers

El barquito
(The Little Boat)

Era una vez un barquito chiquitito,
Era una vez un barquito chiquitito,
Era una vez un barquito chiquitito,
Que no podia, que no podia, que no podia caminar.

Pasaron una, dos, tres, cuatro, cinco, seis, siete, semanas.

Pasaron una, dos, tres, cuatro, cinco, seis, siete, semanas.

Pasaron una, dos, tres, cuatro, cinco, seis, siete, semanas.

Y los víveres y los víveres empezaron a escasear.

Los tripulantes de este barquito,

Los tripulantes de este barquito,

Los tripulantes de este barquito,

Se pusieron, se pusieron, se pusieron a pescar.

Pescaron peces grandes, chicos y medianos,

Pescaron peces grandes, chicos y medianos,

Pescaron peces grandes, chicos y medianos,

Y se pusieron, y se pusieron, y se pusieron a comer.

English Translation

Once upon a time there was a little boat,

Once upon a time there was a little boat,

Once upon a time there was a little boat,

That could not go, that could not go, that could not go.

One week, two, three, four, five, six, seven weeks passed.

One week, two, three, four, five, six, seven weeks passed.

One week, two, three, four, five, six, seven weeks passed.

And the food began to be scarce.

The crew members of that little boat,

The crew members of that little boat,

The crew members of that little boat,

Started fishing, started fishing, started fishing.

They fished big, medium, and small fishes,

They fished big, medium, and small fishes,

They fished big, medium, and small fishes,

And began eating, began eating, and began eating.

And if this story does not seem long to you,

And if this story does not seem long to you,

And if this story does not seem long to you,

We will start it over, we will start it over, we will start it over.

Theme Connections

Boats and Ships
Counting
Fish

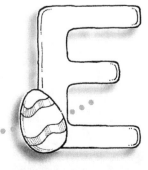

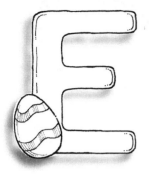

The Elephant Goes

The elephant goes like this, like that. *(move on all fours,
    slowly like an elephant)*
He's terribly big, *(stand up, reach arms high)*
And he's terribly fat. *(stretch arms out to the sides)*
He has no fingers, *(make fists, hiding fingers)*
He has no toes, *(wiggle toes)*
    But goodness gracious,
    What a nose! *(point to nose)*

Theme Connections

Elephants
Humor
Movement
Parts of the Body

Elizabeth, Elspeth, Betsey, and Bess

Elizabeth, Elspeth, Betsey, and Bess,
They all went together to seek a bird's nest;
They found a bird's nest with five eggs in,
They all took one, and left four in.

Theme Connections

Birds
Numbers

Elsie Marley

Elsie Marley's grown so fine,
She won't get up to feed the swine,
But lies in bed 'til eight or nine!
Lazy Elsie Marley.

Theme Connections

Farms
Time of Day
Work

Engine, Engine

Engine, engine, number nine,
Ring the bell when it's time.
O—U—T spells out goes he
Into the middle of the dark blue sea.

Engine, engine, number nine,
Running on Chicago line.
When she's polished, she will shine.
Engine, engine, number nine.

Engine, engine, number nine,
Running on Chicago line.
If the train should jump the track,
Do you want your money back?

Engine, engine, number nine,
Running on Chicago line.
See it sparkle, see it shine,
Engine, engine, number nine.

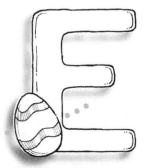

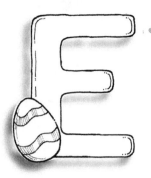

Children sit in a line to form a train, and rock backward and forward to the beat. Do a fast verse as the train gathers speed, and a slow verse as the train comes into the station. When the song ends, toot the whistle, tooooot-toot.

Variation

Engine, engine number nine,
Coming down (your town's) line,
If the train goes off the track
Do you want your money back?
Yes, no, maybe so.

Theme Connections

Money
Numbers
Sounds of Language
Trains

Erie Canal

I've got a mule, her name is Sal,
Fifteen miles on the Erie Canal.
She's a good old worker and a good old pal.
Fifteen miles on the Erie Canal.

We've hauled some barges in our day,
Filled with lumber, coal and hay,
And we know ev'ry inch of the way,
From Albany to Buffalo.

Chorus:
Low bridge, ev'rybody down,
Low bridge, for we're comin' to a town;
And you'll always know your neighbor,
You'll always know your pal,
If you've ever navigated on the Erie Canal.

Git up there, Sal, we passed that lock,
Fifteen miles on the Erie Canal.
And we'll make Rome 'fore six o'clock,
Fifteen miles on the Erie Canal.

Just one more trip and back we'll go,
Through the rain and sleet and snow,
'Cause we know ev'ry inch of the way,
From Albany to Buffalo.

Chorus

Theme Connections

Friends   Transportation
Mules   Weather
Numbers   Work

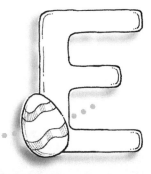

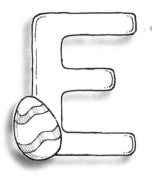

Every Morning at Eight O'Clock

Every morning at eight o'clock,
You can hear the mailman's knock.
Up jumps Katy to open the door,
One letter, two letters, three letters,
Four.

Theme Connections

Counting
Numbers
Occupations
Time of Day

Eye Rhymes

You see me, I see you.
Your eyes are blue. Mine are, too.

Your eyes are big, and round, and brown.
They must be the prettiest eyes in town.

When I look at you, know what I see?
Eyes as green as green can be.

Blue eyes, green eyes,
Brown eyes, hey.

Your eyes are gray,
And I love them that way.

Theme Connections

Colors
Parts of the Body
Self-esteem

Eye Winker

Eye winker, *(point to eye)*
Tom tinker, *(touch ears)*
Nose smeller, *(touch nose)*
Mouth eater, *(touch mouth)*
Chin chopper, *(tap chin)*
Chin chopper, *(tap chin)*
Chin chopper chin. *(tap chin)*

Theme Connections

Parts of the Body

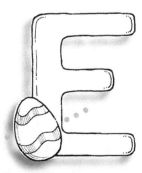

The Family

This is mama, kind and dear. *(point to baby's thumb)*
This is papa, standing near. *(point to pointer finger)*
This is brother, see how tall! *(point to middle finger)*
This is sister, not so tall. *(point to ring finger)*
This is baby, sweet and small. *(point to little finger)*
This is the family one and all. *(wiggle all fingers)*

Theme Connections

Families

Family Fun

Mommy and me dance and sing.
Daddy and me laugh and play.
Mommy, Daddy, and me
Dance and sing,
Laugh and play,
Kiss and hug,
A zillion times a day!

Theme Connections

Emotions
Families

Farmer in the Dell

The farmer in the dell,
The farmer in the dell,
Hi-ho the derry-o,
The farmer in the dell.

The farmer takes a wife…
The wife takes a child…
The child takes a nurse…
The nurse takes a cat…
The cat takes a mouse…
The mouse takes the cheese…
The cheese stands alone…

*Ten children (or more) join hands and dance around the
farmer, who stands in the center of the circle as they sing. At
the end of the first verse, the farmer chooses his wife, who
joins him inside the circle. At the end of the next verse, the
wife takes a child, and so on, until the last verse when everyone is in the cirlcle except the cheese, who stands alone in the
middle of the circle. Whoever winds up being the cheese
becomes the farmer for the next round.*

Theme Connections

Cats
Families
Farms
Mice

Father, Mother, and Uncle John

Father, Mother, and Uncle John
Went to the doctor one by one.
Father fell off,
Mother fell off,
But Uncle John rode on and on.
Father fell off,
Mother fell off,
But Uncle john rode on.

Theme Connections

Families
Occupations

Fiddle-i-Fee

I had a cat, and the cat pleased me.
Fed my cat under yonder tree.
Cat went fiddle-i-fee.

I had a hen, and the hen pleased me.
Fed my hen under yonder tree.
Hen went chimmey chuck, chimmey chuck,
Cat went fiddle-i-fee.

I had a dog, and the dog pleased me.
Fed my dog under yonder tree.
Dog went bow-wow, bow-wow,
Hen went chimmey chuck, chimmey chuck,
Cat went fiddle-I-fee.

Theme Connections

Animal Sounds
Cats
Chickens
Dogs

Fido

I have a little dog
And his name is Fido.
He is nothing but a pup.
He can stand up on his hind legs
If you hold his front legs up.

Theme Connections

Dogs

Firefighters

Up onto their loud, loud truck
  The firefighters climb.
   They're in an awful hurry,
  They move in quick, quick time.
  They're going to put out a fire,
 Help is on the way.
They'll get there with their water hose
And spray and spray and spray.

Theme Connections

Occupations
Transportation

Fire, Fire

"Fire, fire!" said Mrs. McGuire.
"Where, where?" said Mrs. Ware.
"Downtown!" said Mrs. Brown.
"Heaven save us!" said Mrs. Davis.

Theme Connections

Occupations

Five Currant Buns

Five currant buns in the baker's shop,
Big and round with some sugar on the top.
Along came Tom with a penny to pay,
Who bought a currant bun and took it right away.

Four currant buns…
Three currant buns…
Two currant buns…
One currant bun…

No currant buns in the baker's shop,
Big and round with some sugar on the top.
No one came with a penny to pay.
So close the baker's shops and have a baking day.

Theme Connections

Counting
Food
Money
Numbers
Occupations

Five Fingers on Each Hand

I have five fingers on each hand,
Ten toes on my two feet.
Two ears, two eyes,
One nose, one mouth,
With which to sweetly speak.

My hands can clap, my feet can tap,
My eyes can clearly see.
My ears can hear,
My nose can sniff,
My mouth can say, "I'm me."

Theme Connections

Counting
Numbers
Parts of the Body
Self-esteem
Senses

Five Little Ducks

Five little ducks went out one day
Over the hills and far away.
Papa duck called with a
    "Quack, quack, quack."
Four little ducks came swimming back.

*Repeat, losing one more duck each time until you are left
with one duck. Have mama duck call and end with "five little ducks came swimming back."*

Theme Connections

> Animal Sounds
> Counting
> Ducks

Five Little Fingers

One little finger standing on its own. *(hold up index finger)*
Two little fingers, now they're not alone. *(hold up middle finger)*
Three little fingers happy as can be. *(hold up ring finger)*
Four little fingers go walking down the street. *(hold up all fingers)*
Five little fingers. This one is a thumb. *(hold up four fingers and thumb)*
Wave bye-bye 'cause now we are done. *(wave bye-bye)*

Theme Connections

> Counting
> Parts of the Body
> Self-esteem

Five Little Froggies

Five little froggies sitting on a well.
One looked up, and down he fell.
Froggies jumped high,
Froggies jumped low.
Four little froggies sitting on a well.

Four little froggies…
Three little froggies…
Two little froggies…

One little froggy sitting on a well.
He looked up, and down he fell.
Froggies jumped high,
Froggies jumped low.
No little froggies sitting on a well.

Theme Connections

Counting
Frogs
Numbers
Opposites

Variation

Five little froggies sat on a shore. *(crouch like a frog)*
One went for a swim, then there were four. *(one "frog"
    jumps off)*
Four little froggies looked out to sea. *(put hand to brow and
look out to sea)*
One went swimming, then there were three. *(one "frog"
    jumps off)*
Three little froggies said, "What can we do?" *(look puzzled)*
One jumped in the water, then there were two. *(one "frog"
    jumps off)*
Two little froggies sat in the sun. *(crouch like frog)*
One swam off, then there was one. *(one "frog" jumps off)*
One little froggie said, "This is no fun!"
He dived in the water, and then there was none!

Five Little Mice

Five little mice came out to play
Gathering crumbs along the way.
Out came pussycat sleek and fat
Four little mice went scampering back.

Four little mice came out to play
Gathering crumbs along the way.
Out came pussycat sleek and fat
Three little mice went scampering back.

Three little mice came out to play
Gathering crumbs along the way.
Out came pussycat sleek and fat
Two little mice went scampering back.

Two little mice came out to play
Gathering crumbs along the way.
Out came pussycat sleek and fat
One little mouse went scampering back.

One little mouse came out to play
Gathering crumbs along the way.
Out came pussycat sleek and fat
No little mice went scampering back.

Theme Connections

Cats
Counting
Mice
Numbers

Five Little Monkeys
(jumping on the bed)

Five little monkeys jumping on the bed.
One fell off and bumped her head.
Mamma called the doctor, and the doctor said,
"No more monkeys jumping on the bed!"

Repeat, subtracting a monkey each time. Say the rhyme using fingers or act it out.

Theme Connections

Counting
Families
Monkeys
Numbers
Occupations

Five Little Monkeys
(swinging from a tree)

Five little monkeys swinging from a tree,
Teasing Mr. Alligator, you can't catch me.
(whisper) Along comes Mr. Alligator,
   (put palms together and slither hands like an alligator)
Quiet as can be, and
Snapped that monkey right outta that tree.
   (louder, and clap hands on "snapped")

Repeat with 4,3,2,1 monkeys.

Variation

Five little monkeys
Sitting in a tree
Teasing Mr. Crocodile—
"You can't catch me."
"You can't catch me."
Along comes Mr. Crocodile
As quiet as can be—
SNAP!!

Continue until all monkeys are gone.

Away swims Mr. Crocodile
As full as he can be!

Theme Connections

   Alligators
   Counting
   Monkeys
   Numbers

Five Little Pumpkins

Five little pumpkins sitting on a gate. *(hold up five fingers)*
First one said, "Oh my, it's getting late." *(wiggle first finger)*
Second one said, "There's witches in the air." *(wiggle second finger)*
Third one said, "We don't care." *(wiggle third finger)*
Fourth one said, "Let's run, and run, and run." *(wiggle fourth finger)*
Fifth one said, "Oh, it's just Halloween fun." *(wiggle fifth finger)*
But whooo went the wind and out went the light *(hold hands sides of your mouth and blow)*
And five little pumpkins rolled out of sight. *(roll hand over hand)*

Theme Connections

Counting
Holidays
Pumpkins
Sounds of Language

Five Little Sausages

Five little sausages frying in a pan,
   (wiggle all five fingers)
Sizzle, sizzle, sizzle, and one went BAM!

When you reach the "BAM" part of the fingerplay, clap your hands together. Count down with each little sausage (fingers) *until you are out of sausages.*

Variation

Three Little Hot Dogs
   (Place 3 fingers from your right hand onto the palm of your left hand, patting them up and down)
Three little hot dogs frying in the pan,
The pan got hot and one *(hold up 1 finger)* went BAM!
   (clap on "BAM")
   (Place 2 fingers from your right hand onto the palm of your left hand)
Two little hot dogs frying in the pan,
The pan got hot and one *(hold up 1 finger)* went BAM!
   (clap on "BAM")
   (Place 1 fingers from your right hand onto the palm of your left hand)
One little hot dog frying in the pan,
The pan got hot and one *(hold up 1 finger)*
Went, "Wait! Wait! Put me on your plate and eat me up!'

Theme Connections

Counting
Food
Numbers

Five Little Snowmen

Five little snowmen happy and gay,
(hold up five fingers and move one for each snowman)
The first one said, "What a nice day!"
The second one said, "We'll cry no tears."
The third one said, "We'll stay for years."
The fourth one said, "But what happens in May?"
The fifth one said, "Look, we're melting away!"
(hold hands out like saying all gone)

Variation

Five little snowmen fat
Each with a funny hat.
Out came the sun and melted one,
What a sad thing was that…down, down, down.

Repeat with 4, 3, 2, and 1.

Theme Connections

Counting
Numbers
Weather

Five Little Speckled Frogs

(Five children sit in a row and the other children sit in a circle around them. All children act out the words to the song.)

Five little speckled frogs *(hold up five fingers)*

Sitting on a speckled log

Eating some most delicious bugs. *(pretend to eat bugs)*

Yum! Yum!

One jumped into the pool,

   (one child from center jumps back into the circle)

Where it was nice and cool.

   (cross arms over chest and shiver)

Now there are four little speckled frogs.

Burr-ump!

Repeat, counting down until there are no little speckled frogs.

Theme Connections

Counting

Frogs

Five Waiting Pumpkins

(suit actions to words)
Five little pumpkins growing on a vine
First one said, "It's time to shine!"
Second one said, "I love the fall"
Third one said, "I'm round as a ball."
Fourth one said, "I want to be a pie."
Fifth one said, "Let's say good-bye."
"Good-bye," said one!
"Adios," said two!
"Au revoir," said three!
"Ciao," said four!
"Aloha," said five!
And five little pumpkins were picked that day!

Theme Connections

Counting	Numbers
Holidays	Pumpkins
Languages	

Floppy Rag Doll

(suit actions to words)
Flop your arms, flop your feet,
Let your hand go free.
You're the floppiest rag doll
I am ever going to see.

Theme Connections

Movement
Parts of the Body

Flour of England, Fruit of Spain

Flour of England
Fruit of Spain
Met together in a shower of rain.
Put in a bag,
Tied round with a string;
If you'll tell me this riddle,
I'll give you a ring.
(plum pudding)

Theme Connections

> Cooking
> Food

The Fly Hath Married the Bumblebee

Puss came dancing out of the barn
With a pair of bagpipes under her arm.
She could play nothing but Fiddle cum fee
The fly hath married the bumblebee.
Then all of the birds of the air did sing.
Did you ever hear so merry a thing?
Fiddle cum fee, fiddle cum fee
The fly hath married the bumblebee.

Variation

Fiddle dee dee, fiddle dee dee,
The fly has married the bumblebee.
Said the fly, said he,
"Will you marry me,
And live with me sweet bumblebee?"
Fiddle dee dee, fiddle dee dee,
The fly has married the bumblebee.

Theme Connections

Bumblebee
Fly
Humor
Music

Fooba Wooba John

Saw a snail chase a whale,
Fooba Wooba, Fooba Wooba,
Saw a snail chase a whale,
Fooba Wooba John.

Saw a snail chase a whale,
All around the water pail.
Hey, John, ho, John,
Fooba Wooba John.

Saw a frog chase a dog,
Fooba Wooba, Fooba Wooba,
Saw a frog chase a dog,
Sitting on a hollow log.
Hey, John, ho, John,
Fooba Wooba John.

Saw a flea kick a tree,
Fooba Wooba, Fooba Wooba,
Saw a flea kick a tree,
Fooba Wooba John.

Saw a flea kick a tree,
In the middle of the sea.
Hey, John, ho, John,
Fooba Wooba John.

Heard a cow say meow,
Fooba Wooba, Fooba Wooba,
Heard a cow say meow,
Fooba Wooba John.

Heard a cow say meow,
Then I heard it say bow wow.
Hey, John, ho, John,
Fooba Wooba John.

Theme Connections

Cows	Insects
Dogs	Snails
Frogs	Sounds of Language
Humor	Whales

The Food Song
by Jackie Silberg

Capellini, fettucini, escargot, and bok choy.
Jambalaya and papaya, teriyaki, bok choy.
Herring, kippers, guacamole,
Kreplach, crumpets, ravioli,
Gyros, gumbo, sushi, curry, poi, bok choy.

Tacos, baklava, egg rolls.
French fries, rumaki, Sally Lunn.
Bratwurst, lasagna, wonton,
Chow mein, ceviche, crab rangoon.

Theme Connections

Food
Languages
Sounds of Language

Found a Peanut
(Tune: Clementine)

Found a peanut, found a peanut,
Found a peanut just now,
Oh, I just now found a peanut,
Found a peanut just now.

Cracked it open, cracked it open,
Cracked it open just now,
Oh, I just now cracked it open,
Cracked it open just now.

It was rotten…
Ate it anyway…
Got a stomachache…
Called the doctor…
Penicillin…
Operation…
Died anyway…
Went to heaven…
Wouldn't take me…
Went the other way…
Didn't want me…
Was a dream…
Then I woke up…
Found a peanut…

Theme Connections

Food
Humor

Four Seeds

Four seeds in a hole.
Four seeds in a hole.
One for the mouse,
One for the crow,
One to rot and one to grow!

Theme Connections

Birds
Counting
Farms
Growing Things
Mice
Numbers

The Fox Went Out on a Chilly Night

The fox went out on a chilly night
He prayed to the moon to give him light.
For he'd many a mile to go that night
Before he'd reach the town-o, town-o, town-o
He'd many a mile to go that night
Before he reached the town-o.

Theme Connections

Farms
Foxes
Sun, Moon, Stars

Frog Went a-Courtin'

Frog went a-courtin' and he did ride.
Uh-huh; uh-huh.
Frog went a-courtin' and he did ride
With a sword and scabbard by his side.
Uh-huh; uh-huh.

He rode up to Miss Mousie's den.
Uh-huh; uh-huh.
He rode up to Miss Mousie's den,
Said "Please, Miss Mousie, won't you let me in?"
Uh-huh; uh-huh.

"First, I must ask my Uncle Rat.
Uh-huh; uh-huh.
"First I must ask my Uncle Rat
And see what he will say to that."
Uh-huh; uh-huh.

"Miss Mousie, won't you marry me?"
Uh-huh; uh-huh.
"Miss Mousie, won't you marry me
Way down under the apple tree?"
Uh-huh; uh-huh.

"Where will the wedding supper be?"
Uh-huh; uh-huh.
"Where will the wedding supper be?"
 "Under the same old apple tree."
Uh-huh; uh-huh.

"What will the wedding supper be?"
Uh-huh; uh-huh.
"What will the wedding supper be?"
"Hominy grits and black-eyed peas."
Uh-huh; uh-huh.

The first come in was a bumblebee.
Uh-huh; uh-huh.
The first come in was a bumblebee
With a big bass fiddle on his knee.
Uh-huh; uh-huh.

The last come in was a mockingbird.
Uh-huh; uh-huh.
The last come in was a mockingbird
Who said, "This marriage is absurd."
Uh-huh; uh-huh.

Theme Connections

Families
Frogs
Humor
Mice

A Froggie Sat on a Log

A froggie sat on a log,
A-weeping for his daughter.
His eyes were red,
His tears he shed,
And he fell right into the water.

Theme Connections

Emotions
Families
Frogs
Parts of the body

From Wibbleton

From Wibbleton to Wobbleton is 15 miles.
From Wobbleton to Wibbleton is 15 miles.
From Wibbleton to Wobbleton, from Wobbleton to
    Wibbleton,
From Wibbleton to Wobbleton is 15 miles.

Theme Connections

Numbers
Sounds of Language
Transportation

Frosty Weather

Frosty weather, snowy weather,
When the wind blows,
We all go together.

Theme Connections

Weather

Fuzzy Wuzzy
Was a Bear

Fuzzy Wuzzy was a bear.
Fuzzy Wuzzy had no hair.
Fuzzy Wuzzy wasn't fuzzy
Was he?

Theme Connections

Bears
Humor

Ghost of John

Have you seen the ghost of John?
Long white bones and the rest all gone.
Ooh, ooh, ooh, ooh.
Wouldn't we be chilly with no skin on?

Theme Connections

Holidays
Parts of the Body

Giddy Up

Giddy up, giddy up, one, two, three.
Giddy up, giddy up, come see me.

Theme Connections

Counting
Horses
Numbers

Go In and Out the Window

Go round and round the village,
Go round and round the village,
Go round and round the village,
As we have done before.

Go in and out the window,
Go in and out the window,
Go in and out the window,
As we have done before.

Now stand and face your partner,
Now stand and face your partner,
Now stand and face your partner,
As we have done before.

Now follow her to London,
Now follow her to London,
Now follow her to London,
As we have done before.

Now shake his hand and leave him,
Now shake his hand and leave him,
Now shake his hand and leave him,
As we have done before.

Verse 1: One or two children go to the center of a circle of
children, who are holding hands up high.
The selected children thread in and out of the circle through
the other children's arms.
Verse 2: The children in the center pick partners by stopping
in front of another child.
Verse 3: The chosen children follow their partners as they
thread in and out of the circle.

Verse 4: All the children join hands and circle in one direction.

Variation

Go round and round the village,
Go round and round the village,
Go round and round the village,
As we have done before.

Go in and out the window,
Go in and out the window,
Go in and out the window,
As we have done before.

Now stand and face your playmates,
Now stand and face your playmates,
Now stand and face your playmates,
As we have done before.

Now shake hands with your partner,
Now shake hands with your partner,
Now shake hands with your partner,
As we have done before.

Now take her (him) off to London,
Now take her (him) off to London,
Now take her (him) off to London,
As we have done before.

Theme Connections

Opposites
Movement
Spatial Relationships

Go Tell Aunt Rhody

Go tell Aunt Rhody,
Go tell Aunt Rhody,
Go tell Aunt Rhody
The old gray goose is dead.

The one she's been saving,
The one she's been saving,
The one she's been saving
To make a feather bed.

The goslings are mourning,
The goslings are mourning,
The goslings are mourning
Because their mother's dead.

The old gander's weeping,
The old gander's weeping,
The old gander's weeping,
Because his wife is dead.

She died in the mill pond,
She died in the mill pond,
She died in the mill pond
From standing on her head.

Go tell Aunt Rhody,
Go tell Aunt Rhody,
Go tell Aunt Rhody
The old gray goose is dead.

Theme Connections

Emotions
Families
Geese

Go to Bed Early

Go to bed early—wake up with joy;
Go to bed late—cross girl or boy.
Go to bed early—ready for play;
Go to bed late—moping all day.
Go to bed early—no pains or ills;
Go to bed late—doctors and pills.
Go to bed early—grow very tall.
Go to bed late—stay very small.

Theme Connections

Growing Up
Naptime/Sleeping
Opposites

Gobble, Gobble, Gobble

Gobble, gobble, gobble,
Quack, quack, quack,
A turkey says gobble,
And a duck says quack.

Theme Connections

Animal Sounds
Ducks
Holidays
Turkeys

Going on a Bear Hunt

(Leader says a line—others repeat. Pat on thighs in rhythm.)
Would you like to go on a bear hunt?
Okay—all right—come on—let's go!
Open the gate—close the gate. *(clap hands)*

Coming to a bridge—can't go over it—can't go under it.
Let's cross it. *(thump chest with fists)*

Coming to a river—can't go over it—can't go under it.
Let's swim it. *(swim)*

Coming to a tree—can't go over it—can't go under it.
Let's climb it. *(climb up)*
No bears! *(climb down)*

Coming to a wheat field—can't go over it—can't go under it.
Let's go through it! *(rub palms together to make swishing
    noise)*

Oh! Oh! I see a cave—it's dark in here. *(cover eyes)*
I see two eyes—I feel something furry. *(reach out hand)*
It's a bear!
Let's go home! *(run in place)*
    *(Describe and repeat above actions in reverse using fast
    motions)*
Slam the gate! *(clap hands)*
We made it!

Theme Connections

Bears
Emotions
Rivers
Spatial Relationships

Gold Ships

There are gold ships.
There are silver ships.
But there's no ship
Like a friendship.

Theme Connections

Boats and Ships
Friends

Good Morning

Good morning to you!
Good morning to you!
We're all in our places
With bright shining faces.
Oh, this is the way to start a great day!

Theme Connections

Emotions
Sun, Moon, Stars
Time of Day

Good noontime to you!
Good noontime to you!
We're all in our places
With food on our faces.
Oh, this is the way to have a great day!

Good evening to you!
Good evening to you!
Stars and moon in their places
They go through their paces.
Oh, this is the way to end a good day!

Good Morning, Merry Sunshine

Good morning, merry sunshine,
How did you wake so soon?
You've scared the little stars away,
And shone away the moon.
I watched you go to sleep last night,
Before I stopped my play,
How did you get way over there,
And, pray, where did you stay?

I never go to sleep, dear,
I just go 'round to see
My little children of the East,
Who rise to watch for me.
I waken all the birds and bees,
And flowers on my way,
Then last of all, the little child
Who stayed out late to play.

Theme Connections

Opposites
Sun, Moon, Stars
Time of Day

Good Morning, Mrs. Hen

Good morning, Mrs. Hen
How many chickens have you got?
Madam, I've got ten;
Four of them are yellow,
Four of them are brown,
And two of them are speckled red,
The nicest in the town.

Theme Connections

Chickens
Colors
Counting
Numbers

Good Night, Sleep Tight

Good night, sleep tight,
Wake up bright,
In the morning light,
To do what's right,
With all your might.

Theme Connections

Naptime/Sleeping
Time of Day

Goosey, Goosey, Gander

Goosey, goosey, gander,
Whither shall I wander?
Upstairs, and downstairs,
And in my lady's chamber.

Theme Connections

Geese
Opposites

Grand Old Duke of York

The grand old Duke of York *(salute)*
He had ten thousand men. *(hold up ten fingers)*
He marched them up to the top of the hill, *(point up)*
And he marched them down again. *(point down)*
And when they're up, they're up. *(stand tall)*
And when they're down, they're down. *(squat)*
But when they're only halfway up, *(stoop down)*
They're neither up nor down. *(open arms and shrug)*

Theme Connections

Movement
Numbers
Opposites

Grandpa's (or Grandma's) Glasses

These are Grandpa's glasses. *(make glasses with fingers)*
This is Grandpa's hat. *(tap head)*
This is how he folds his hands, *(fold hands)*
And puts them in his lap. *(place hands in lap)*

Variation

Here are Grandma's spectacles, *(make circles with thumbs
  and index fingers and place over eyes)*
And here is Grandma's hat. *(join hands at fingertips and
  place on top of head)*
And here's the way she holds her hands, *(fold hands)*
And puts them in her lap. *(place folded hands gently in lap)*

Here are Grandpa's spectacles, *(make circles with thumbs
  and index fingers and place them over eyes)*
And here is Grandpa's hat. *(make larger pointed hat, as above)*
And here's the way he folds his arms, *(fold arms with vigor)*
And sits like that. *(sit down hard)*

Theme Connections

Clothing
Families
Parts of the Body

Granfa' Grig

Grandfa' Grig
Had a pig
In a field of clover;
Piggy died,
Grandfa' cried
And all the fun was O-VER.

Theme Connections

Emotions
Families
Pigs

Gray Goose and Gander

Gray goose and gander,
Waft your wings together,
And carry the good king's daughter
Over the one-strand river.

Theme Connections

Geese
Kings and Queens
Rivers

Gray Squirrel

Gray squirrel, gray squirrel, *(stand with hands on bent knees)*
Swish your bushy tail.
  (wiggle your behind)
Gray squirrel, gray squirrel,
  (stand with hands on bent knees)
Swish your bushy tail. *(wiggle your behind)*
Wrinkle up your funny nose, *(wrinkle nose)*
Hold an acorn in your toes.
  (pinch index and thumb fingers together)
Gray squirrel, gray squirrel, *(stand with hands on bent knees)*
Swish your bushy tail. *(wiggle your behind)*

Theme Connections

Colors
Seasons
Squirrels

Green Cheese

Green cheese,
Yellow laces,
Up and down
The marketplaces.

Theme Connections

Colors
Opposites

Green Grass Grew All Around

In the park there was a hole,
Oh, the prettiest hole you ever did see.
A hole in the park,
A hole in the ground,
And the green grass grew all around, all around,
And the green grass grew all around.

And in that hole there was a sprout,
Oh, the prettiest sprout you ever did see.
Sprout in the hole,
Hole in the ground,
And the green grass grew all around, all around,
And the green grass grew all around.

And from that sprout there grew a tree,
Oh, the prettiest tree you ever did see.
Tree from a sprout,
Sprout in a hole,
Hole in the ground,
And the green grass grew all around, all around,
And the green grass grew all around.

And on that tree there was a branch,
Oh, the prettiest branch you ever did see.
Branch on a tree,
Tree from a sprout,
Sprout in a hole,
Hole in the ground,
And the green grass grew all around, all around,
And the green grass grew all around.

And on that branch there was a nest,
Oh, the prettiest nest you ever did see.

Nest on a branch,
Branch on a tree,
Tree from a sprout,
Sprout in a hole,
Hole in the ground,
And the green grass grew all around, all around,
And the green grass grew all around.

And in that nest there was an egg,
Oh, the prettiest egg you ever did see.
Egg in a nest,
Nest on a branch,
Branch on a tree,
Tree from a sprout,
Sprout in a hole,
Hole in the ground,
And the green grass grew all around, all around,
And the green grass grew all around.

And in that egg there was a bird,
Oh, the prettiest bird you ever did see.
Bird in an egg,
Egg in a nest,
Nest on a branch,
Branch on a tree,
Tree from a sprout,
Sprout in a hole,
Hole in the ground,
And the green grass grew all around, all around,
And the green grass grew all around.

Theme Connections

Birds
Colors
Growing Things
Nature

Green Grow the Rushes O

I will sing you one O
Green grow the rushes O
What is your one O
One is one and all alone
And evermore shall be so

I will sing you two O
Green grow the rushes O
What is your two O
Two, two the lily white boys
Clothed all in green O

I will sing you three O
Green grow the rushes O
What is your three O

Three, three the rivals
Four, for the gospel makers
Five for the symbols at your door
Six for the six proud walkers
Seven for the seven stars in the sky
Eight for the April rainers
Nine for the nine bright shiners
Ten for the Ten Commandments
Eleven for the eleven that went to heaven
Twelve for the twelve apostles

Theme Connections

Colors
Counting
Numbers

Gregory Griggs

Gregory Griggs, Gregory Griggs,
Had twenty-seven different wigs.
He wore them up, he wore them down
To please the people of the town.
He wore them east,
He wore them west,
But he never could tell which one he loved best.

Theme Connections

Numbers
Opposites
Spatial Relationships

Had a Little Rooster

Had a little rooster by the barnyard gate.
That little rooster was my playmate.
That little rooster went cock-a-doodle-doo,
Dee-doodle-dee, doodle-dee, doodle-dee-doo.

Had a little cat by the barnyard gate,
That little cat was my playmate,
That little cat went meow, meow, meow,
That little rooster went cock-a-doodle-doo,
Dee-doodle-dee, doodle-dee, doodle-dee-doo.

Had a little dog by the barnyard gate.
That little dog was my playmate.
That little dog went arf, arf, arf,
That little cat went meow, meow, meow,
That little rooster went cock-a-doodle-doo,
Dee-doodle-dee, doodle-dee, doodle-dee-doo.

Had a little duck by the barnyard gate,
That little duck was my playmate,
That little duck went quack, quack, quack,
That little dog went arf, arf, arf,
That little cat went meow, meow, meow,
That little rooster went cock-a-doodle-doo,
Dee-doodle-dee, doodle-dee, doodle-dee-doo.

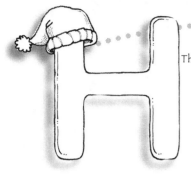

Had a little pig by the barnyard gate,
That little pig was my playmate,
That little pig went oink, oink, oink,
That little duck went quack, quack, quack,
That little dog went arf, arf, arf,
That little cat went meow, meow, meow,
That little rooster went cock-a-doodle-doo,
Dee-doodle-dee, doodle-dee, doodle-dee-doo.

Had a little sheep by the barnyard gate,
That little sheep was my playmate,
That little sheep went baa, baa, baa,
That little pig went oink, oink, oink,
That little duck went quack, quack, quack,
That little dog went arf, arf, arf,
That little cat went meow, meow, meow,
That little rooster went cock-a-doodle-doo,
Dee-doodle-dee, doodle-dee, doodle-dee-doo.

Had a little cow by the barnyard gate,
That little cow was my playmate,
That little cow went moo, moo, moo,
That little sheep went baa, baa, baa,
That little pig went oink, oink, oink,
That little duck went quack, quack, quack,
That little dog went arf, arf, arf,
That little cat went meow, meow, meow,
That little rooster went cock-a-doodle-doo,
Dee-doodle-dee, doodle-dee, doodle-dee-doo.

Had a little horse by the barnyard gate,
That little horse was my playmate,
That little horse went neigh, neigh, neigh,
That little cow went moo, moo, moo,
That little sheep went baa, baa, baa,
That little pig went oink, oink, oink,
That little duck went quack, quack, quack,
That little dog went arf, arf, arf,

That little cat went meow, meow, meow,
That little rooster went cock-a-doodle-doo,
Dee-doodle-dee, doodle-dee, doodle-dee-doo.

Variation

I had a rooster and the rooster pleased me.
I fed my rooster on the green berry tree.
My little rooster went...

Theme Connections

Animal Sounds	Ducks	Pigs
Cats	Farms	Roosters
Cows	Horses	Sheep
Dogs		

Handy Pandy

Handy Pandy, Jack-a-dandy,
Loves plum cake and sugar candy.
He bought some at the grocer's shop
And out he came, hop, hop, hop.

Little Jack-a-dandy,
Has a stick of candy.
Every time he takes a bite
A piece goes quickly out of
    sight.
Happy, happy, Jack-a-Dandy.
Yum, yum, yum, yum, yum

Variation

Handy Spandy Jack-a-dandy
Loves carrot cake and chocolate candy.
He bought some at the grocery store
And he was happy ever more.

Handy Spandy sugary candy
French almond rock:
Bread and butter for your supper
That is all your mother's got.

Theme Connections

Food
Money
Occupations

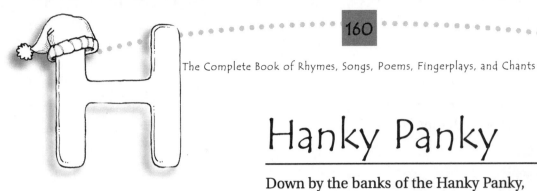

Hanky Panky

Down by the banks of the Hanky Panky,
Where the bullfrogs jump from bank to banky
With an Eep! Eep! Ope! Ope!
Knee flop-i-dilly and ker-plop.

Theme Connections

Frogs
Sounds of Language

He's Got the Whole World in His Hands

He's got the whole world in His hands,
He's got the whole world in His hands,
He's got the whole world in His hands,
He's got the whole world in His hands.

He's got my brothers and my sisters in His hands,
He's got my brothers and my sisters in His hands,
He's got my brothers and my sisters in His hands,
He's got the whole world in His hands.

He's got the sun and the rain in His hands,
He's got the moon and the stars in His hands,
He's got the wind and the clouds in His hands,
He's got the whole world in His hands.

He's got the rivers and the mountains in His hands,
He's got the oceans and the seas in His hands,
He's got you and he's got me in His hands,
He's got the whole world in His hands.

He's got everybody here in His hands,
He's got everybody there in His hands,
He's got everybody everywhere in His hands,
He's got the whole world in His hands.

Theme Connections

Families
Nature
Sun, Moon, Stars

Head and Shoulders

Head, shoulders, knees and toes
Knees and toes
Head, shoulders, knees and toes
Knees and toes
Eyes and ears and mouth and nose
Head, shoulders, knees and toes
Knees and toes.

Variation

(Tune: London Bridge)
Head and shoulders, knees and toes, *(touch the body parts named)*
Knees and toes, knees and toes,
Head and shoulders, knees and toes,
Eyes, ears, mouth, and nose.

Theme Connections

Movement
Parts of the Body

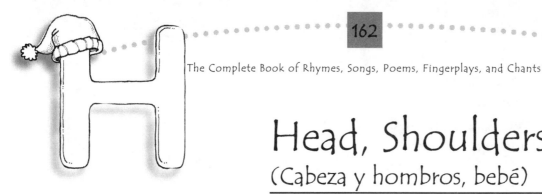

Head, Shoulders, Baby
(Cabeza y hombros, bebé)

Head, shoulders, baby 1, 2, 3.
Head, shoulders, baby 1, 2, 3.
Head, shoulders, head, shoulders,
Head, shoulders, baby 1, 2, 3.

Shoulders, hip, baby, 1, 2, 3.
Shoulders, hip, baby, 1, 2, 3.
Shoulders, hip, shoulders, hip,
Shoulders, hip, baby, 1, 2, 3.

Hip, knees.
Knees, ankle.
Ankle, toes.
Toes, ankle.
Ankle, knees.
Knees, hips.
Hip, shoulders.
Shoulders, head.

Spanish Translation

Cabeza y hombros, bebé
Cabeza y hombros, bebé 1, 2, 3.
Cabeza y hombros, bebé 1, 2, 3.
Cabeza y hombros, bebé 1, 2, 3.
Cabeza, hombros, cabeza, hombres,
Cabeza y hombros, bebé 1, 2, 3.

Hombros, caderas, bebé, 1, 2, 3.
Hombros, caderas, bebé, 1, 2, 3.
Hombros, caderas, bebé, 1, 2, 3.
Hombros, caderas, hombros, caderas
Hombros, caderas, bebé, 1, 2, 3.

—caderas, rodillas.

—rodillas, tobillos.

—tobillos, dedos.

—dedos, tobillos.

—tobillos, rodillas.

—rodillas, caderas.

—caderas, hombres.

—hombros, cabeza.

Theme Connections

Counting

Numbers

Parts of the Body

Hear the Lively Song

Hear the lively song
Of the frogs in yonder pond.
Crick, crick, crickety-crick,
Burr-ump!

Theme Connections

Animal Sounds

Frogs

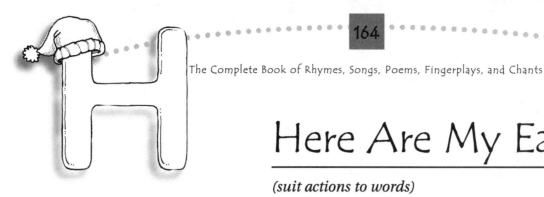

Here Are My Ears

(suit actions to words)
Here are my ears.
Here is my nose.
Here are my fingers.
Here are my toes.

Here are my eyes
Both open wide.
Here is my mouth
With white teeth inside.

Here is my tongue
That helps me speak.
Here is my chin
And here are my cheeks.

Here are my hands
That help me play.
Here are my feet
For walking today.

Theme Connections

Parts of the Body
Self-esteem

Here Are My Eyes

Here are my eyes, *(point to eyes)*
One and two.
I can wink. *(wink)*
So can you.

When my eyes are open, *(open eyes wide)*
I see the light.
When they are closed, *(close eyes)*
It's dark as night.

Theme Connections

Parts of the Body
Self-esteem

Here Is a Beehive

Here is a beehive. *(make a beehive with fists)*
Where are the bees? *(pretend to look around for them)*
Hiding inside *(try to see inside the beehive)*
Where nobody sees!

Soon they come creeping *(unlock fists slowly)*
Out of the hive.
One, two, three, four, five!

Theme Connections

Bees
Counting
Numbers

Variation

Here is the beehive, where are the bees? *(clench fist)*
Hidden away where nobody sees.
Watch and you will see them come out of their hives,
One, two, three, four, five, *(bring out fingers quickly one by one)*
Buzz, buzz, buzz.

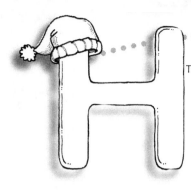

Here Is a Bunny

Here is a bunny with ears so funny, *(bend two fingers over thumb)*
And here is a hole in the ground. *(make hole with left hand)*
When a noise he hears, he pricks up his ears, *(hold "ears" straight)*
And hops into his hole so round. *(hop bunny over into the "hole")*

Variation

This is the bunny with ears so funny, *(hold fingers to make bunny ears)*
And this is his hole in the ground. *(shape fingers of other hand like a hole in the ground)*
When a noise he hears, he pricks up his ears,
And then jumps in his hole so round. *(use appropriate motion)*

Theme Connections

Rabbits

Here Is a House

Here is a house built up high, *(stretch arms up touching fingertips like a roof)*
With two tall chimneys reaching the sky. *(stretch arms up separately)*
Here are the windows. *(make a square shape with your hands)*
Here is the door. *(knock)*
If we peep inside
We'll see a mouse on the floor. *(move fingers like a running mouse)*

Theme Connections

Houses and Homes
Mice
Movement

Here Is the Sea

Here is the sea, the wavy sea. *(wave your hands from side to side)*
Here is my boat, *(cup your hands like a boat)*
And here is me. *(point to yourself)*
All of the fishes *(wiggle your fingers)*
Down below *(point downward)*
Wiggle their tails, *(wiggle your fingers)*
And away they go. *(wiggle your fingers behind your back)*

Theme Connections

Boats and Ships
Fish
Oceans and Seas

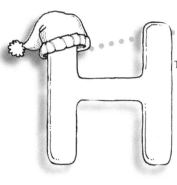

Here Sits the Lord Mayor

Here sits the Lord Mayor. *(touch forehead)*
Here sit his men. *(touch eyes)*
Here sits the cockadoodle. *(touch right cheek)*
Here sits the hen. *(touch left cheek)*
Here sit the little chickens. *(tap teeth)*
Here they run in, *(touch mouth)*
Chin chopper, chin chopper
Chin chopper chin. *(touch chin)*

Theme Connections

Chickens
Parts of the Body

Here We Come Gathering Knots of May

Here we come gathering knots of May,
Knots of May, knots of May.
Here we come gathering knots of May,
At six o'clock in the morning.

Theme Connections

Months of the Year
Seasons
Time of Day

Here We Go

Here we go—up, up, up. *(stand up on toes)*
Here we go—down, down, down. *(crouch down)*
Here we go—moving forward. *(take a step forward)*
Here we go—moving backward. *(take a step backward)*
Here we go round and round and round. *(spin)*

Theme Connections

Opposites
Spatial Relationships

Hey, Diddle, Diddle, Dout

Hey, diddle, diddle, dout,
My candle's out,
My little maid's not at home;
Saddle the hog,
And bridle the dog,
And fetch my little maid home.

Home she came,
Trittity trot,
She asked for the porridge she left in the pot;
Some she ate,
And some she shod,
And some she gave to the trucker's dog.

Theme Connections

Dogs
Food
Pigs

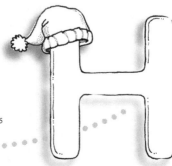

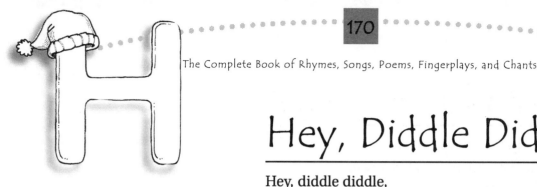

Hey, Diddle Diddle

Hey, diddle diddle,
The cat and the fiddle,
The cow jumped over the moon.
The little dog laughed to see such a sight,
And the dish ran away with the spoon.

Theme Connections

Cats
Cows
Dogs
Humor
Sun, Moon, Stars

Hey, Diddle Dinkety Poppety Pet

Hey, diddle dinkety poppety pet
The merchants of London they wear scarlet.
Silk in the collar and gold in the hem
So merrily march the merchant men.

Theme Connections

Colors
Occupations

Hey, My Name Is Joe!

Hey, my name is Joe!
I have a wife, one kid, and I work in a button factory.
One day, my boss said, "Are you busy?"
I said, "No."
"Then turn a button with your right hand." *(make a turning gesture with right hand)*

Hey, my name is Joe!
I have a wife, two kids, and I work in a button factory.
One day, my boss said, "Are you busy?"
I said, "No."
"Then turn a button with your left hand." *(make a turning gesture with left hand as you continue with the right hand)*

(Continue adding number of children and adding right and left feet and head.)

Hey, my name is Joe!
I have a wife, six kids and I work in a button factory.
One day, my boss said, "Are you busy?"
I said, "Yes!"

Theme Connections

Families
Humor
Parts of the Body
Work

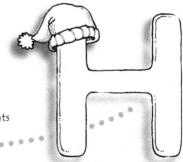

Hickety, Pickety, My Black Hen

Hickety, pickety, my black hen,
She lays eggs for gentlemen.
Gentlemen come every day
To see what my black hen doth lay.
Sometimes nine and sometimes ten,
Hickety, pickety, my black hen.

Theme Connections

Chickens
Colors
Counting
Numbers

Hickory, Dickory, Dock

Hickory, dickory, dock, *(stand, swing arm like pendulum)*
The mouse ran up the clock. *(bend over; run hand up body)*
The clock struck one, *(clap hands over head once)*
The mouse ran down, *(run hand down to feet)*
Hickory, dickory, dock. *(stand; swing arm like pendulum)*

Theme Connections

Mice
Time of Day

Higglety, Pigglety, Pop!

Higglety, pigglety, pop!
The dog has eaten the mop;
The pig's in a hurry,
The cat's in a flurry,
Higglety, pigglety, pop!

Theme Connections

Cats
Dogs
Humor
Pigs

High and Low

I reach my hands way up high. *(reach high)*
I can almost touch sky.
Then I bend way down low, *(touch the floor)*
And touch the floor just so.

Theme Connections

Opposites
Spatial Relationships

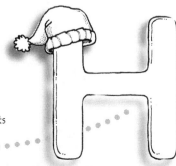

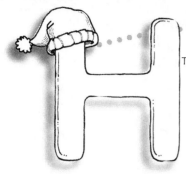

High There in the Deep Blue Sky

High there in the deep blue sky,
Down the Milky Way,
Rides a ship without a sail,
With no oars, they say.
White the ship, its only crew
Is a rabbit white.
Westward they're floating onward,
Quietly through the night.

Theme Connections

Boats and Ships
Colors
Nature
Rabbits
Sun, Moon, Stars

Hinx, Minx

Hinx, minx the old witch winks,
The fat begins to fry.
Nobody's home but Jumping Joan,
Father, mother and I.

Theme Connections

Families
Food
Holidays

Hippity Hop to the Grocery Shop

Hippity hop to the grocery shop
To buy three sticks of candy.
One for you and one for me,
And one for sister Mandy.

Theme Connections

Candy
Counting
Families
Occupations

Hokey Pokey

(suit actions to words)
You put your right hand in,
You put your right hand out,
You put your right hand in,
And you shake it all about. *(wiggle)*
You do the Hokey Pokey
And you turn yourself around,
That's what it's all about.

Continue with other verses that put in other parts of the body and finish up with your whole self!

Theme Connections

Movement
Parts of the Body

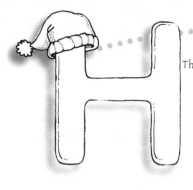

Home on the Range
by Brewster Higley

Oh, give me a home where the buffalo roam,
Where the deer and the antelope play.
Where seldom is heard a discouraging word,
And the skies are not cloudy all day.

Chorus:
Home, home on the range,
Where the deer and the antelope play.
Where seldom is heard a discouraging word
And the skies are not cloudy all day.

How often at night when the heavens are bright
With the light from the glittering stars,
Have I stood there amazed and asked as I gazed
If their glory exceeds that of ours.

Chorus

Where the air is so pure, the zephyrs so free
The breezes so balmy and light.
That I would not exchange my home on the range
For all of the cities so bright.

Chorus

Oh, I love those wild flow'rs in this dear land of ours
The curlew, I love to hear scream.
And I love the white rocks and the antelope flocks
That graze on the mountaintops green.

Chorus

Theme Connections

Antelope
Colors
Cowboys
Cowgirls
Deer
Nature
Sun, Moon, Stars

Home, Sweet Home

'Mid pleasure and palaces though we may roam,
Be it ever so humble, there's no place like home.

A charm from the skies seems to hallow us there,
Which seek through the world, is ne'er met with elsewhere.

Home! Home! Sweet, sweet home!
Be it ever so humble, there's no place like home.

Theme Connections

Houses and Homes

Horsie, Horsie

Horsie, horsie, don't you stop.
Just let your feet go clippety clop.
Your tail goes swish and the wheels go round,
Giddyup, you're homeward bound.

Theme Connections

Horses
Houses and Homes
Transportation

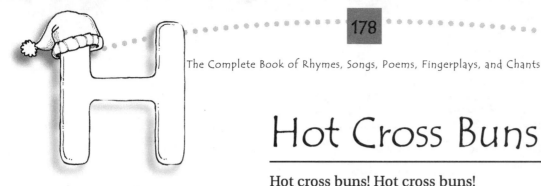

Hot Cross Buns!

Hot cross buns! Hot cross buns!
One a penny, two a penny,
Hot cross buns!
If your daughters do not like them
Give them to your sons.
But if you haven't any
Of these pretty little elves,
You cannot do better
Than eat them yourselves.

Theme Connections

Counting   Food
Families   Money

The House That Jack Built

This is the house that Jack built.

This is the malt
That lay in the house that Jack built.

This is the rat,
That ate the malt,
That lay in the house that Jack built.

This is the cat,
That killed the rat,
That ate the malt,
That lay in the house that Jack built.

This is the dog,
That worried the cat,
That killed the rat,
That ate the malt,
That lay in the house that Jack built.

This is the cow with the crumpled horn,
That tossed the dog,
That worried the cat,
That killed the rat,
That ate the malt,
That lay in the house that Jack built.

This the maiden all forlorn,
That milked the cow with the crumpled horn,
That tossed the dog,
That worried the cat,
That killed the rat,
That ate the malt,
That lay in the house that Jack built.

This is the man all tattered and torn,
That kissed the maiden all forlorn,
That milked the cow with the crumpled horn,
That tossed the dog,
That worried the cat,
That killed the rat,
That ate the malt,
That lay in the house that Jack built.

This is the priest all shaven and shorn,
That married the man all tattered and torn,
That kissed the maiden all forlorn,
That milked the cow with the crumpled horn,
That tossed the dog,
That worried the cat,
That killed the rat,
That ate the malt,
That lay in the house that Jack built.

This is the cock that crowed in the morn,
That waked the priest all shaven and shorn,
That married the man all tattered and torn,
That kissed the maiden all forlorn,
That milked the cow with the crumpled horn,

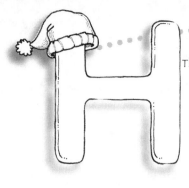

That tossed the dog,
That worried the cat,
That killed the rat,
That ate the malt,
That lay in the house that Jack built.

This is the farmer sowing his corn,
That kept the cock that crowed in the morn,
That waked the priest all shaven and shorn,
That married the man all tattered and torn,
That kissed the maiden all forlorn,
That milked the cow with the crumpled horn,
That tossed the dog,
That worried the cat,
That killed the rat,
That ate the malt,
That lay in the house that Jack built.

Theme Connections

Animals
Farms
Houses and Homes

How Go the Ladies

How go the ladies, how go they?
Amble, amble all the way.
How go the lords and gentlemen?
Trit, trot, trit and home again.
How goes the farmer, how goes he?
Hobble de gee, hobble de gee.
How goes the butcher boy who longs to be rich?
A gallop, a-gallop, a-gallop,
A plonk in the ditch.

Theme Connections

Horses
Sounds of Language

How Many Miles to Babylon?

How many miles to Babylon?
Three score miles and ten.
Can I get there by candle-light?
Yes, and back again.
If your heels are nimble and light,
You may get there by candle-light.

Variation

How many miles to London town?
Three score and ten;
Can I get there by candlelight?
Yes, and back again.

Theme Connections

Numbers
Time of Day

How Much Wood

How much wood would a woodchuck chuck
If a woodchuck could chuck wood?
He would chuck what wood a woodchuck would chuck
If a woodchuck would chuck wood.

Theme Connections

Humor
Sounds of Language
Woodchucks

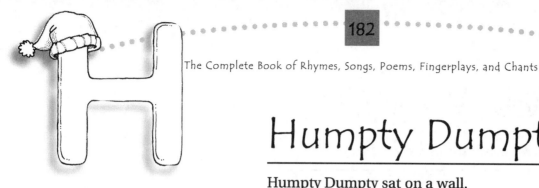

Humpty Dumpty

Humpty Dumpty sat on a wall.
Humpty Dumpty had a great fall.
All the king's horses and all the king's men
Couldn't put Humpty Dumpty together again.

Variation

Humpty Dumpty sat on a wall,
Humpty Dumpty had a great fall.
Four score men and four score more
Cannot put Humpty Dumpty where he was before.

Humpty Dumpty and his brother
Were as like as one another.
Couldn't tell one from t'other
Humpty Dumpty and his brother.

Humpty Dumpty sat on a spoon
Humpty will go in the egg cup soon.
    And all the paste and all the glue
    Willl not make Humpty look like new.

Theme Connections

Humor
Kings and Queens

A-Hunting We Will Go

Oh, a-hunting we will go, a-hunting we will go!
We'll catch a little fox and put him in a box
And then we'll let him go.

…fish…put him in a dish…
…bear…cut his hair…
…pig…dance a jig…
…giraffe…make him laugh…

Theme Connections

Animals	Foxes	Pigs
Bears	Giraffes	
Fish	Humor	

Hush, Little Baby

Hush, little baby, don't say a word.
Mama's gonna show you a mockingbird.
If that mockingbird won't sing,
Mama's gonna show you a diamond ring.
If that diamond ring turns brass,
Mama's gonna show you a looking glass.
If that looking glass gets broke,
Mama's gonna show you a billy goat.
If that billy goat won't pull,
Mama's gonna find you a cart and bull.
If that cart and bull turn over,
Mama's gonna bring you a dog named Rover.
If that dog named Rover won't bark,
Mama's gonna find you a horse and cart.
If that horse and cart fall down,
You'll still be the sweetest little baby in town.

Theme Connections

Babies
Families
Lullabies
Naptime/Sleeping

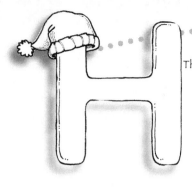

Hush-a-Bye

Hush-a-bye, don't you cry,
Go to sleep you little baby.
When you wake, you shall have
All the pretty little horses.
Dapples and greys, tans and bays,
All the pretty little horses.

Variation

Hush-a-bye, don't you cry
Go to sleep little baby.
Blacks and bays, dapples and grays,
Coach and six-a-little horses.
Hush-a-bye, don't you cry
Go to sleep little baby.

Theme Connections

Babies
Horses
Lullabies
Naptime/Sleeping

I Can Do It Myself

Hat on head, just like this
Pull it down, you see.
I can put my hat on
All by myself, just me.

One arm in, two arms in,
Buttons, one, two, three.
I can put my coat on
All by myself, just me.

Toes in first, heels down next,
Pull and pull, then see—
I can put my boots on
All by myself, just me.

Fingers here, thumbs right here,
Hands warm as can be.
I can put my mittens on
All by myself, just me.

Theme Connections

Clothing   Seasons
Parts of the Body   Self-esteem

I Clap My Hands

(suit actions to words)
I clap my hands,
I touch my feet,
I jump up from the ground.
I clap my hands,
I touch my feet,
And turn myself around.

Theme Connections

Parts of the Body
Self-esteem

I Clap My Hands
(to make a sound)

I clap my hands to make a sound—
Clap, clap, clap!
I tap my toe to make a sound—
Tap, tap, tap!

I open my mouth to say a word—
Talk, talk, talk!
I pick up my foot to take a step—
Walk, walk, walk!

Theme Connections

Parts of the Body
Self-esteem

I Eat My Peas

I eat my peas with honey.
I've done it all my life.
It makes the peas taste funny,
But it keeps them on the knife.

Theme Connections

Food
Humor

I Had a Dog

I had a dog and his name was Dandy,
His tail was long and his legs were bandy.
His eyes were brown and his coat was sandy,
The best in the world was my dog Dandy.

Theme Connections

Colors
Dogs
Emotions

I Had a Little Brother

I had a little brother
No bigger than my thumb;
I put him in the coffee pot
Where he rattled like a drum.

Theme Connections

Families
Humor

I Had a Little Cow

I had a little cow
Hey-diddle, ho-diddle.
I had a little cow, and it had a little calf.
Hey-diddle, ho-diddle and there's my song half.

I had a little cow
Hey-diddle, ho-diddle.
I had a little cow and I drove it to the stall.
Hey-diddle, ho-diddle and there's my song all.

Theme Connections

Cows
Farms
Sounds of Language

I Had a Little Dog

I had a little dog and his name was Bluebell;
I gave him some work and he did it very well.
I sent him upstairs to pick up a pin;
He stepped in the coal scuttle up to his chin.
I sent him to the garden to pick some sage;
He tumbled down and fell in a rage.
I sent him to the cellar to draw a pot of beer;
He came up again and said there was none there.

Theme Connections

Dogs
Humor
Work

I Had a Little Pig

I had a little pig and fed him in a trough.
He got so fat his tail dropped off.
So I got me a hammer and I got me a nail,
And I made my piggie a brand new tail.

Theme Connections

Humor
Pigs

I Had a Little Pony
(his name was Dapple Gray)

I had a little pony,
His name was Dapple Gray.
I lent him to a lady
To ride a mile away.
She whipped him, she lashed him,
She rode him through the mire.
I would not lend my pony now,
For all the lady's hire.

Theme Connections

Emotions
Horses

I Had a Little Pony
(that trotted up and down)

I had a little pony
That trotted up and down.
I bridled him and saddled him
And trotted out of town.

Theme Connections

Horses
Opposites
Transportation

I Had a Loose Tooth

I had a loose tooth,
A wiggly, jiggly loose tooth.
I had a loose tooth,
A-hanging by a thread.

I pulled my loose tooth,
My wiggly, jiggly loose tooth.
Put it 'neath my pillow,
And then I went to bed.

The fairy took my loose tooth,
My wiggly, jiggly loose tooth.
And now I have a quarter,
And a hole in my head.

Theme Connections

Humor
Growing Up
Money
Naptime/Sleeping
Teeth

I Have a Little Sister

I have a little sister, they call her Peep, Peep;
She wades the waters deep, deep, deep;
She climbs the mountains high, high, high;
Poor little creature, she has but one eye. (a star)

Theme Connections

Naptime/Sleeping
Sun, Moon, Stars

I Have a Little Wagon

I have a little wagon. *(hold hand out palm up)*
It goes everywhere with me. *(move hand around)*
I can pull it, *(pull hand toward you)*
I can push it, *(push hand away from you)*
 I can turn it upside down. *(turn hand upside down)*

Theme Connections

Opposites
Toys

I Have So Many Parts to Me

I have two hands to clap with, *(clap)*
One nose with which to smell. *(sniff)*
I have one head to think with, *(tap head)*
Two lungs that work quite well. *(take a deep breath)*
I have two eyes that let me see, *(point to eyes)*
I have two legs that walk. *(walk)*

Theme Connections

Movement
Numbers
Parts of the Body
Senses

I Have Something in My Pocket

I have something in my pocket.
It belongs across my face.
I keep it very close at hand
In a most convenient place.

I bet you could guess it,
If you guessed a long, long while.
So I'll take it out and put it on,
It's a great big happy SMILE!

Theme Connections

Humor
Parts of the Body

I Have Two Eyes

I have two eyes to see with,
I have two feet to run,
I have two hands to wave with,
And nose I have but one.
I have two ears to hear with,
And a tongue to say "Good day."

Theme Connections

Numbers
Parts of the Body
Senses

I Know a Little Puppy

I know a little puppy; he hasn't any tail.
He isn't very chubby; he's skinny as a rail.
Although he is a puppy, he'll never be a hound.
They sell him at the shop for 30 cents a pound.
Bow-wow, wow-wow, wow-wow, wow.
HOT DOG!

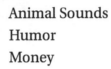

Theme Connections

Animal Sounds
Humor
Money

I Know a Little Pussy

I know a little pussy; her coat is silver gray.
She lives down in the meadow not very far away.
Although she is a pussy, she'll never be a cat,
For she's a pussywillow. What do you think of that?
Meow, meow, meow, meow, meow, meow, meow!

Theme Connections

Animal Sounds
Colors
Humor
Nature

Variation

I have a little pussy
Her coat is silver gray.
She lives in a great wide meadow,
And she never runs away.

She always is a pussy;
She'll never be a cat.
Because she's a pussywillow,
Now what do you think of that!

I Know Something

I know something I won't tell.
Three little monkeys in a peanut shell.
One can read and one can write,
And one can smoke a corncob pipe.

Theme Connections

Counting
Humor
Monkeys

I Like Silver

I like silver.
I like brass.
I like looking
In the looking-glass.
I like rubies.
I like pearls.
I like wearing
My hair in curls.

Theme Connections

Self-esteem

I Love Little Pussy

I love little pussy.
Her coat is so warm,
And if I don't hurt her
She'll do me no harm.
So I'll not pull her tail,
Nor drive her away.
But pussy and I,
Very gently will play.

Theme Connections

Cats

I Love the Mountains

I love the mountains.
I love the rolling hills.
I love the flowers.
I love the daffodils.
Boom-de-otta, boom-de-otta, boom-de-otta, boom-de-otta.

Theme Connections

Nature
Sounds of Language

I Measure Myself

(suit actions to words)
I measure myself from my head to my toes,
I measure my arms, starting right by my nose.
I measure my legs and I measure me all,
I measure to see if I'm growing tall.

Theme Connections

Growing Up
Parts of the Body
Self-esteem

I Never Had a Dog

I never had a dog that could talk,
Or a cat that could sing a song,
Or a pony that could on two legs walk,
And keep it up all the day long.

Or a pig that could whistle a merry tune,
Or a hen that could dance a jig,
Or a cow that could jump clear over the moon,
Or a musical guinea pig.

Theme Connections

Animals
Humor

I Never Saw a Purple Cow

I never saw a purple cow.
I never hope to see one.
But I can tell you anyhow
I'd rather see than be one.

Theme Connections

Colors
Cows
Humor

I Saw a Ship a-Sailing

I saw a ship a-sailing,
  A-sailing on the sea;
  And, Oh! It was all laden
  With pretty things for thee!

There were comfits in the cabin,
And apples in the hold.
The sails were made of silk,
And the masts were made of gold.

The four-and-twenty sailors
That stood between the decks,
Were four-and-twenty white mice,
With chains about their necks.

The captain was a duck
With a packet on her back.
And when the ship began to move,
The captain said, "Quack! Quack!"

Theme Connections

Animal Sounds
Apples
Boats and Ships
Colors
Ducks
Mice
Numbers

I Saw Eight Magpies

I saw eight magpies in a tree.
Two for you and six for me.
One for sorrow, two for mirth.
Three for a wedding, four for a birth.
Five for England, six for France.
Seven for a fiddler, eight for a dance.

Theme Connections

Birds
Counting
Numbers

I Stand on Tiptoe

I stand on tiptoe
To make myself tall.
I bend my knees
To make myself small.
But now I like my sit-down size best of all!

Theme Connections

Opposites
Self-esteem

I Use My Brain

by Jackie Silberg

I use my brain to think, think, think.
I use my nose to smell.
I use my eyes to blink, blink, blink.
I use my throat to yell.
I use my mouth to giggle, giggle, giggle.
I use my hips to bump.
I use my toes to wiggle, wiggle, wiggle,
And I use my legs to jump.

Theme Connections

Humor   Parts of the Body
Movement   Self-esteem

I Went Upstairs
(just like me)

I went upstairs,
Just like me.
I looked into the mirror,
Just like me.
Saw a little monkey,
Just like me.

Theme Connections

Humor
Monkeys
Self-esteem

I Went Upstairs
(to make my bed)

I went upstairs to make my bed,
And by mistake I bumped my head.

I went downstairs to cook my food,
And by mistake I cooked my shoe.

I went downstairs to hang some clothes,
And by mistake I hung my toes.

I went downstairs to milk my cow,
And by mistake I milked the sow.

I went into the kitchen to bake a pie,
And by mistake I baked a fly.

Theme Connections

Clothing
Food
Humor
Self-esteem

I Wiggle

I wiggle, wiggle, wiggle my fingers. *(wiggle fingers)*
I wiggle, wiggle, wiggle my toes. *(wiggle toes)*
I wiggle, wiggle, wiggle my shoulders. *(wiggle shoulders)*
I wiggle, wiggle, wiggle my nose. *(wiggle nose)*
Now no more wiggles are left in me, *(shake head)*
I am sitting as still as still can be. *(sit still)*

Theme Connections

Movement
Parts of the Body

I Wish I Were
(Tune: If You're Happy and You Know It)

Oh, I wish I were a little juicy orange, juicy orange.
Oh, I wish I were a little juicy orange, juicy orange.
I'd go squirty, squirty, squirty
Over everybody's shirty.
Oh, I wish I were a little juicy orange, juicy orange.

Oh, I wish I were a little bar of soap, bar of soap.
Oh, I wish I were a little bar of soap, bar of soap.
I'd go slidy, slidy, slidy
Over everybody's body.
Oh, I wish I were a little bar of soap, bar of soap.

Oh, I wish I were a little blob of mud, blob of mud.
Oh, I wish I were a little blob of mud, blob of mud.
I'd go gooey, gooey, gooey
Over everybody's shoey.
Oh, I wish I were a little blob of mud, blob of mud.

Oh, I wish I were a little cookie crumb, cookie crumb.

Oh, I wish I were a little cookie crumb, cookie crumb.

I'd go crumby, crumby, crumby

Over everybody's tummy.

Oh, I wish I were a little cookie crumb, cookie crumb.

Oh, I wish I were a little radio, radio.

Oh, I wish I were a little radio, radio.

I'd go CLICK!

Theme Connections

Humor

If All the Seas

If all the seas were one sea

What a great sea it would be!

And if all the trees were one tree

What a great tree it would be!

And if all the axes were one axe,

What a great axe that would be!

And if all the men were one man,

What a great man he would be!

And if the great man took the great axe,

And cut down the great tree,

And if this tree were to fall into the sea,

My, what a splish-splash there would be!

Alternative Ending

And let it fall into the great sea,

What a great splish-splash that would be!

Theme Connections

Humor

Oceans and Seas

If All the World Were Paper

If all the world were paper,
And all the sea were ink,
If all the trees
Were bread and cheese,
What should we have to drink?

Theme Connections

Food
Humor
Nature

If I Had a Donkey

If I had a donkey and he wouldn't go,
D'you think I'd wallop him?
Oh, no, no!
I'd put him in the barn,
And give him some corn,
The best little donkey that ever was born.

Theme Connections

Donkey
Emotions
Kindness

If I Were an Apple

If I were an apple and grew on a tree,
I think I'd drop down on a nice child like me.
I wouldn't stay there giving nobody joy;
I'd fall down at once and say, "Eat me, my boy."

Theme Connections

Apples
Nature

If Wishes Were Horses

If wishes were horses,
Beggars would ride;
If turnips were watches,
I would wear one by my side.

Variation

If wishes were horses, beggars would ride.
If turnips were watches, I would wear one by my side.
And if "ifs" and "ands" were pots and pans,
There'd be no work for tinkers!

Theme Connections

Horses
Humor

If You're Happy and You Know It

If you're happy and you know it, clap your hands.
  (clap hands twice)
If you're happy and you know it, clap your hands.
  (clap hands twice)
If you're happy and you know it, then your face will surely
  show it. *(point to face)*
If you're happy and you know it, clap your hands.
  (clap hands twice)

If you're happy and you know it, stomp your feet.
  (stomp feet twice)
If you're happy and you know it, stomp your feet.
  (stomp feet twice)
If you're happy and you know it, then your face will surely
  show it. *(point to face)*
If you're happy and you know it, stomp your feet.
  (stomp feet twice)

If you're happy and you know it, shout "Hurray!"
  (shout "hurray!")
If you're happy and you know it, shout "Hurray!"
  (shout "hurray!")
If you're happy and you know it, then your face will surely
  show it.
If you're happy and you know it, shout "Hurray!"
  (shout "Hurray!")

If you're happy and you know it, do all three.
  (clap hands twice, stomp feet twice, shout "Hurray!")
If you're happy and you know it, do all three.
  (clap hands twice, stomp feet twice, shout "Hurray!")
If you're happy and you know it, then your face will surely
  show it.
If you're happy and you know it, do all three.
  (clap hands twice, stomp feet twice, shout "Hurray!")

Si Estás Contento
Si estás contento y lo sabes, aplaudirás.
Si estás contento y lo sabes, aplaudirás.
Si estás contento y lo sabes, tu cara lo mostrará.
Si estás contento y lo sabes, aplaudirás.

Theme Connections

Emotions
Parts of the Body

I'll Buy You a Tartan Bonnet

I'll buy you a Tartan bonnet,
And feathers to put on it.
With a hush-a-bye and a lullaby,
Because you are so like your daddy.

Theme Connections

Babies
Emotions
Families
Naptime/Sleeping

I'm a Choo-Choo Train

I'm a choo-choo train *(bend arms at side)*
Chugging down the track. *(rhythmically move arms)*
First I go forward, *(move forward)*
Then I go back. *(move backward)*

Now my bell is ringing. *(pretend to pull bell)*
Hear my whistle blow.
What a lot of noise I make *(cover ears)*
Everywhere I go!

Theme Connections

Opposites
Sounds
Trains

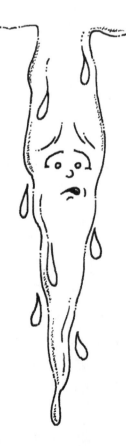

I'm a Frozen Icicle

I'm a frozen icicle
Hanging by your door.
When it's cold, I grow some more.
When it's warm, I'm on the floor!

Theme Connections

Opposites
Seasons

I'm a Jack-o-Lantern

I'm a Jack-o'-Lantern with a great big grin. *(smile)*

I'm a Jack-o'-Lantern with a candle in. *(hold index finger in front of mouth)*

Poof! goes the wind and *(blow quickly at finger)*

Out goes the light. *(shut eyes)*

Away fly the witches *(flap arms)*

Out of sight.

Theme Connections

Holidays

Pumpkins

I'm a Little Acorn Brown

I'm a little acorn brown,

Lying on the cold, cold ground.

Everyone walks over me,

That is why I'm cracked you see.

I'm a nut (click, click).

In a rut (click, click).

I'm a nut (click, click).

In a rut (click, click).

Theme Connections

Colors

Seasons

I'm a Little Dutch Girl

(suit actions to words)
I'm a little Dutch girl dressed in blue.
Here are the things I like to do:
Salute to the captain, bow to the queen,
Turn my back on the submarine.
I can do the tap dance,
I can do the split,
I can do the holka polka
Just like this.

Theme Connections

Colors
Kings and Queens
Movement

In a Cabin in the Woods

In a cabin in the woods, *(outline imaginary cabin)*
A little man by the window stood,
(circle fingers for eye glasses)
Saw a rabbit hopping by *(bounce hands in front of you)*
Frightened as could be. *(simulate fright)*
Help me! Help me! Help me! he said,
(throw hands up in the air)
Or the hunter will bump my head! *(tap head)*
Come little rabbit, come with me;
(motion "come")
Happy we will be. *(pat hand)*

Theme Connections

Emotions
Movement
Rabbits

In a Cottage in Fife

In a cottage in Fife,
Lived a man and his wife,
Who, believe me were comical folk.
For, to people's surprise,
They both saw with their eyes,
And their tongues moved whenever they spoke.
When quite fast asleep,
I've been told that to keep
Their eyes open they could not contrive.
They walked on their feet,
And 'twas thought what they eat
Helped with drinking to keep them alive.

Theme Connections

Families
Humor
Parts of the Body
Senses

In Marble Walls

In marble walls as white as milk,
Lined with a skin as soft as silk,
Within a fountain crystal clear,
A golden apple doth appear;
No doors there are to this stronghold,
Yet thieves break in and steal the gold.
(an egg)

Theme Connections

Colors
Humor

Inside Out

When I'm happy on the inside,
It shows on the outside.
It is quiet impossible you see,
To hide what's inside of me.

When I am happy, I dance.
I lift my feet and prance.
I twirl and spin and glide.

Theme Connections

Emotions
Movement

It Rains, It Blows

It rains, it hails, it batters, it blows
And I am wet through all my clothes
I prithee, love, let me in!

Theme Connections

Weather

It's Raining

It's raining, it's pouring,
The old man is snoring,
He went to bed and he bumped his head
And he couldn't get up in the morning.

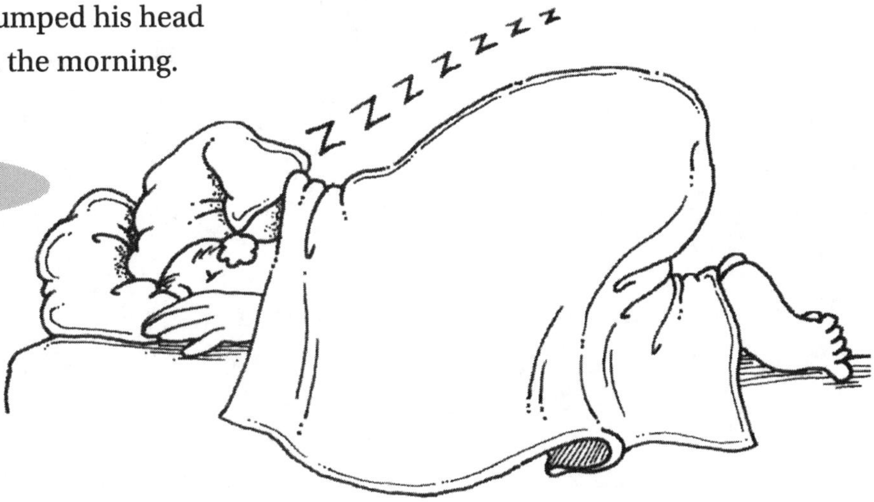

Theme Connections

Naptime
Sleeping
Time of Day
Weather

Itsy Bitsy Spider

The itsy bitsy spider
Went up the water spout.
Down came the rain
And washed the spider out.
Out came the sun
And dried up all the rain.
And the itsy bitsy spider
Went up the spout again.

Theme Connections

Spatial Relationships
Spiders
Sun, Moon, Stars
Weather

I've Been Working on the Railroad

I've been workin' on the railroad,
All the live long day.
I've been workin' on the railroad,
Just to pass the time away.
Don't you hear the whistle blowing?
Rise up so early in the morn.
Don't you hear the captain shouting
Dinah, blow your horn?

Dinah, won't you blow,
Dinah, won't you blow,
Dinah, won't you blow your horn?
Dinah, won't you blow,
Dinah, won't you blow,
Dinah, won't you blow your horn?

Someone's in the kitchen with Dinah.
Someone's in the kitchen, I know.
Someone's in the kitchen with Dinah
Strumming on the old banjo.

Fee, fie, fiddle-e-i-o.
Fee, fie, fiddle-e-i-o-o-o-o.
Fee, fie, fiddle-e-i-o.
Strumming on the old banjo.

Theme Connections

Music
Sounds of Language
Trains
Work

I've Got Sixpence

I've got sixpence, jolly, jolly, sixpence,
I've got sixpence to last me all my life.
I've got two pence to spend and two pence to lend
And two pence to take home to my wife, poor wife!

Chorus:
No cares have I to grieve me
No pretty little girls to deceive me
I'm as happy as a lark, believe me
As we go rolling, rolling home.
Rolling home (rolling home),
Rolling home (rolling home),
As we go rolling, rolling home.

I've got four pence, jolly, jolly, four pence,
I've got four pence to last me all my life.
I've got two pence to spend and four pence to lend
And no pence to take home to my wife, poor wife!

Chorus

Theme Connections

Emotions
Families
Money
Numbers

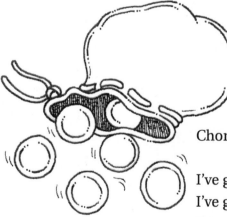

I've got two pence, jolly, jolly, two pence,
I've got two pence to last me all my life.
I've got two pence to spend and no pence to lend
And no pence to take home to my wife, poor wife!

Chorus

I've got no pence, jolly, jolly, no pence,
I've got no pence to last me all my life.
I've got no pence to spend and no pence to lend
And no pence to take home to my wife, poor wife!

Chorus

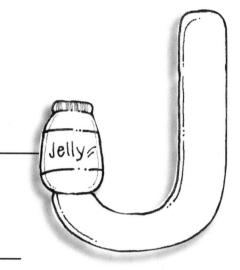

Jack and Jill

Jack and Jill
Went up the hill
To fetch a pail of water.
Jack fell down
And broke his crown,
And Jill came tumbling after.

Up Jack got
And home did trot
As fast as he could caper.
Went to bed
And plastered his head
With vinegar and brown paper.

Theme Connections

Families
Houses and Homes
Spatial Relationships
Work

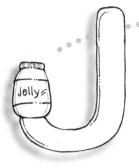

Jack-a-Nory

I'll tell you a story
About Jack-a-Nory,
And now my story's begun;
I'll tell you another
About his brother,
And now my story is done!

Theme Connections

Families
Humor

Jack Be Nimble

Jack be nimble,
Jack be quick;
Jack jump over
The candlestick.

Variation

Jack be nimble, *(tap sticks to beat)*
Jack be quick,
Jack jumped over the candlestick.
Jack jumped high, *(tap sticks over head)*
Jack jumped low,
Jack jumped over and burnt his toe.

Theme Connections

Movement
Spatial Relationships

Jack Frost

Jack Frost bites your noses.
He chills your cheeks and freezes your toes.
He comes every year when winter is here
And stays until spring is near.

Theme Connections

Parts of the Body
Seasons

Jack-in-the-Box

I'm Jack-in-the-box.
I'm Jack-in-the-box.
I crunch so very low.
Turn the handle
Round and round and up I go.
I'm Jack in the box.
I'm Jack in the box.
Just turn the handle and up I pop.

Theme Connections

Opposites
Toys

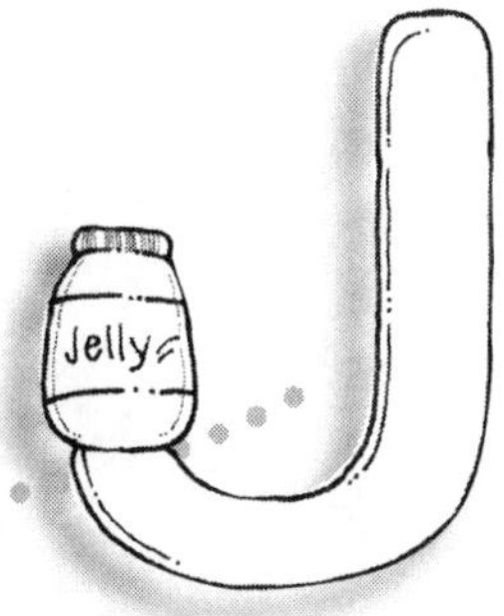

Jack-in-the-Box
(oh, so still)

Jack-in-the-box *(tuck thumb into fist)*
Oh, so still.
Won't you come out? *(raise hand slightly)*
Yes, I will. *(pop thumb out of fist)*

Theme Connections

> Opposites
> Toys

Jack, Jack

Jack, Jack, down you go, *(crouch down low)*
Down in your box, down so low.
Jack, Jack, there goes the top. *(pop up)*
Quickly now, up you pop.

Theme Connections

> Movement
> Opposites
> Spatial Relationships

Jack-o-Lantern
(Tune: Clementine)

Jack-o-lantern, Jack-o-lantern,
You are such a funny sight.
As you sit there in my window
Looking out into the night.

You were once a yellow pumpkin
Growing on a sturdy vine.
Now you are my Jack-o-lantern.
Let your candlelight shine.

Theme Connections

Holidays
Pumpkins

Jack Sprat

Jack Sprat could eat no fat.
His wife could eat no lean.
And so between the two of them
They made the platter clean.

Theme Connections

Families
Food
Opposites

Jaybird, Jaybird

Jaybird, jaybird, sitting on a fence,
Trying to make a dollar out of fifteen cents.

Theme Connections

Birds
Money

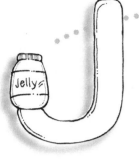

Jelly on the Plate

Jelly on the plate,
Wiggle-waggle, wiggle-waggle,
Jelly on the plate.

Sausage in the pan, sausage in the pan,
Turn it round, turn it round,
Sausage in the pan.

Paper on the floor, paper on the floor,
Pick it up, pick it up,
Paper on the floor.

Theme Connection

Food

Jennie Jenkins

Will you wear white, oh my dear, oh my dear?
Will you wear white, Jennie Jenkins?
No, I won't wear white for the color's too bright.
I'll buy me a fol-de-rol-dy, til-de-tol-dy
Seek-a-double, use-a-cause-a, roll-a-find-me
Roll, Jennie Jenkins, roll.

Will you wear blue, oh my dear, oh my dear?
Will you wear blue, Jennie Jenkins?
No, I won't wear blue 'cause blue won't do.
I'll buy me a fol-de-rol-dy, til-de-tol-dy
Seek-a-double, use-a-cause-a, roll-a-find-me
Roll, Jennie Jenkins, roll.

Will you wear red, oh my dear, oh my dear?
Will you wear red, Jennie Jenkins?
No, I won't wear red, it's the color of my head.
I'll buy me a fol-de-rol-dy, til-de-tol-dy
Seek-a-double, use-a-cause-a, roll-a-find-me
Roll, Jennie Jenkins, roll.

Will you wear pink, oh my dear, oh my dear?
Will you wear pink, Jennie Jenkins?
No, I won't wear pink, I'd rather drink ink.
I'll buy me a fol-de-rol-dy, til-de-tol-dy
Seek-a-double, use-a-cause-a, roll-a-find-me
Roll, Jennie Jenkins, roll.

Will you wear green, oh my dear, oh my dear?
Will you wear green, Jennie Jenkins?
No, I won't wear green, it's the color of a bean.
I'll buy me a fol-de-rol-dy, til-de-tol-dy
Seek-a-double, use-a-cause-a, roll-a-find-me
Roll, Jennie Jenkins, roll.

Will you wear rose, oh my dear, oh my dear?
Will you wear rose, Jennie Jenkins?
No, I won't wear rose, it's the color of my nose.
I'll buy me a fol-de-rol-dy, til-de-tol-dy
Seek-a-double, use-a-cause-a, roll-a-find-me
Roll, Jennie Jenkins, roll.

Theme Connections

Colors
Sounds of Language

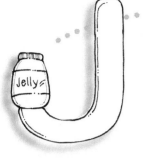

Jim Along Josie

Hey Jim along now
Jim along Josie
Hey Jim along now
Jim along Joe
repeat
Walking along now
Jim along Josie
Walking along now
Jim along Joe
repeat
Creeping along now…
Jumping along now…
Hopping along now…
Tiptoe along now…

Theme Connections

Movement

Jingle Bells/Casca beles

Dashing through the snow
In a one-horse open sleigh
O'er the fields we go
Laughing all the way
Bells on bobtail ring
Making spirits bright
What fun it is to ride and sing
A sleighing song tonight!

Chorus:
Oh! Jingle bells, jingle bells,
Jingle all the way!
Oh, what fun it is to ride
In a one-horse open sleigh!
Hey!
Jingle bells, jingle bells
Jingle all the way!
Oh, what fun it is to ride
In a one-horse open sleigh!

A day or two ago
I thought I'd take a ride;
And soon Miss Fannie Bright
Was seated by my side.
The horse was lean and lank;
Misfortune seemed his lot;
He got into a drifted bank,
And we, we got upsot.

Chorus

Now the ground is white,
Go it while you're young;
Take the girls tonight,
And sing this sleighing song.
Just get a bobtailed bay,
Two-forty for his speed;
Then hitch him to an open sleigh,
And crack! You'll take the lead.

Chorus

Translation

Casca Beles
Casca beles, casca beles,
Hoy es Navidad.
Es un día de a legria y felicidad.
Casca beles, casca beles,
Hoy es Navidad.
Es un día de a legria y felicidad

Theme Connections

    Holidays
    Horses
    Transportation
    Weather

John Brown's Baby

John Brown's baby had a cold upon his chest
John Brown's baby had a cold upon his chest
John Brown's baby had a cold upon his chest
And they rubbed it with camphorated oil.

Verse 2: Omit word "baby" throughout and do motion.
Verse 3: Omit "baby" and "cold" and do motions.
Verse 4: Omit "baby," "cold," and "chest" and do motions.
Verse 5: Omit "baby," "cold," "chest," and "rubbed" and do motions.
Verse 6: Omit "baby," "cold," "chest," "rubbed," and "camporated oil" and do motions.

Motions: (Not done in Verse 1)
baby—pretend to rock baby in arms
cold—sneeze
chest—slap chest
rubbed—rub chest
camphorated oil—hold nose and make a face

Theme Connections

Families
Humor
Movement

John Jacob Jingleheimer Schmidt

John Jacob Jingleheimer Schmidt
His name is my name, too!
Whenever we go out,
The people always shout
There goes John Jacob Jingleheimer Schmidt!
Da da da da da da da

Repeat verse again and again, each time more quietly, but shout loudly on the "Da da da da da da da" line.

Theme Connections

Humor
Opposites
Sounds of Language

Johnny Appleseed

Oh, the earth is good to me,
And so I thank the earth,
For giving me the things I need:
The sun, the rain, and the apple seed.
The earth is good to me.

Theme Connections

Apples   Sun, Moon, Stars
Nature   Weather

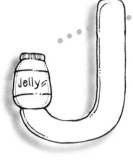

Johnny Works With One Hammer

Johnny works with one hammer,
One hammer, one hammer.
   (make hammering motion with right hand)
Johnny works with one hammer,
Then he works with two.

Johnny works with two hammers…
   (motion with left and right hands)
Johnny works with three hammers…
   (motion with both hands and right foot)
Johnny works with four hammers…
   (motion with both hands and both feet)
Johnny works with five hammers…
   (motion with both hands and feet and with head)
Then he goes to bed.

Theme Connections

Counting
Movement
Numbers
Work

Juba This and Juba That

Juba this; Juba that;
Juba chased a yellow cat.
Juba up; Juba down;
Juba runnin' all around.

Theme Connections

Colors
Opposites
Spatial Relationships

Jumping Joan

Here I am, little jumping Joan.
When nobody's with me,
I'm always alone.

Theme Connection

Movement

Knock at the Door

Knock at the door. *(tap forehead)*
Peek in. *(point to eyes)*
Lift the latch *(touch end of nose)*
And walk in. *(walk fingers from chin to mouth)*
Go way down in the cellar and eat *(pat stomach)*
Up all the apples.

Variation

Knock at the door. *(tap forehead)*
Pull the bell. *(gently pull a lock of hair)*
Lift the latch *(touch tip of nose)*
And walk in. *(touch lip)*

Theme Connections

Apples
Movement
Parts of the Body

Kookaburra

Kookaburra* sits in the old gum tree,
Merry, merry king of the bush is he.
Laugh, Kookaburra! Laugh, Kookaburra!
Gay your life must be.

Kookaburra sits in the old gum tree,
Eating all the gum drops he can see.
Stop, Kookaburra! Stop, Kookaburra!
Leave some there for me.

Kookaburra sits in the old gum tree,
Counting all the monkeys he can see.
Stop, Kookaburra! Stop, Kookaburra!
That's not a monkey, that's me!

Kookaburra sits on a rusty nail,
Gets a boo-boo in his tail.
Cry, Kookaburra! Cry, kookaburra!
Oh, how life can be.

Theme Connections

Birds
Emotions
Monkeys
Nature

* This song was written in 1936, and introduced at a Scout
Jamboree in Melbourne, Australia. A kookaburra is an
Australian bird, and a "gum tree" is what Americans know
as a eucalyptus. The "gum drops" that the kookaburra eats
in the song are beads of the resinous sap.

Kumbaya

Kumbaya, my Lord,
Kumbaya
Kumbaya, my Lord,
Kumbaya
Kumbaya, my Lord,
Kumbaya
Oh, Lord,
Kumbaya.

Someone's cryin', Lord
Kumbaya.
Someone's cryin', Lord
Kumbaya.
Someone's cryin', Lord
Kumbaya.
Oh, Lord,
Kumbaya.

Someone's sighin', Lord…
Someone's laughin', Lord…

Repeat first verse.

Theme Connections

Emotions
Peace

Ladybug! Ladybug!

Ladybug! Ladybug!
Fly away home.
Your house is on fire
And your children all gone.
All except one,
And that's little Ann,
For she has crept under
The frying pan.

Theme Connections

Houses and Homes
Ladybugs

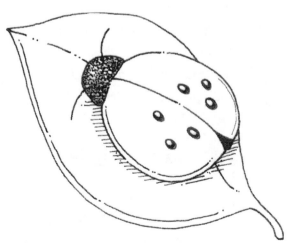

Last Night, the Night Before

Last night, the night before,
A lemon and a pickle came knocking at my door;
I went down to let them in, a-a-and,
They hit me on the head with a rolling pin.

Theme Connection

Humor

Lavender's Blue

Lavender's blue, dilly, dilly,
Lavender's green,
When I am king, dilly, dilly,
You shall be queen.
Call up your men, dilly, dilly,
Set them to work,
Some to the plough, dilly, dilly,
Some to the cart.
Some to make hay, dilly, dilly,
Some to cut corn,
While you and I, dilly, dilly,
Keep ourselves warm.

Theme Connections

Colors
Kings and Queens
Work

Lazy Mary

Lazy Mary, will you get up,
Will you get up, will you get up?
Lazy Mary, will you get up
This cold and frosty morning?

Theme Connections

Naptime/Sleeping
Time of Day
Weather

Leg Over Leg

Leg over leg as the dog went to Dover.
When he came to a stile—
Whoops!
He went over.

Theme Connections

Dogs
Humor

Let's Be Friends

by Jackie Silberg

Chorus:
Lets be friends with one another - (3x)
Let's be friends today.

You can smile at a friend...
Repeat
You can wave to a friend...
Repeat
You can wink at a friend...
Repeat
Let's be friends today

(Chorus)

Theme Connections

Friends   Self-esteem

Let's Go to the Wood

Let's go to the wood," said this little pig.
"What to do there?" said this little pig. *(wiggle each wrist)*
"Find our mother," said this little pig.
"What to do with her?" said this little pig. *(then wiggle each ankle)*
"Kiss her all over," said this little pig. *(pick up the child and kiss and hug her all over)*

Theme Connections

Families   Pigs

Little Arabella Miller

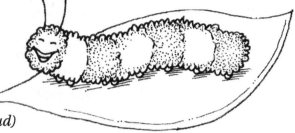

Little Arabella Miller
Had a fuzzy caterpillar.
First it crawled upon her mother,
Then upon her baby brother.
They said, "Arabella Miller
Put away that caterpillar!" *(said quickly and loud)*

Little Arabella Miller
Had a great big green snake. *(ss-ss-s-s)*
First it crawled upon her mother,
Then upon her baby brother.
They said, "Arabella Miller,
Put away that great big green snake!" *(said quickly and loud)*

…orange dragon…
…brontosaurus dinosaur…

Variation

Little Arabella Stiller found a wooly caterpillar.
First it crawled up on her mother,
Then up on her baby brother.
All said, "Arabella Stiller, take away that caterpillar."

Theme Connections

Colors
Families
Humor

Little Ball

A little ball, *(make a circle with your fingers)*
A bigger ball, *(make a circle with your hands)*
A great big ball I see. *(make a circle with your arms)*

Are you ready to count them?

One, *(make a circle with your fingers)*
Two, *(make a circle with your hands)*
Three. *(make a circle with your arms)*

Variation

A great big ball *(arms make circle over head)*
A middle-sized ball, *(make ball with both hands in front)*
A little ball I see. *(make ball with thumb and forefinger)*
Now let's count the balls we've made: 1—2—3 *(make each
    ball again as you count)*

Theme Connections

Balls
Counting
Numbers
Toys

Little Betty Blue

Little Betty Blue lost her holiday shoe.
What can little Betty do?
Give her another
To match the other,
And then she can walk out in two.

Theme Connections

Clothing
Colors
Numbers

Little Bo Peep

Little Bo Peep has lost her sheep,
And can't tell where to find them;
Leave them alone, and they'll come home,
Wagging their tails behind them.

Then she took her little crook,
Determined for to find them;
What a joy to behold them nigh,
Wagging their tails behind them.

Theme Connections

Emotions
Farms
Sheep
Work

Little Boy Blue

Little Boy Blue, come blow your horn,
The sheep's in the meadow, the cow's in the corn.
Where's the little boy that looks after the sheep?
He's under the haystack, fast asleep.

Variation

Little Boy Blue, come blow your horn,
The sheep's in the meadow, the cow's in
the corn.
Where is the boy that looks after the
sheep?
He's under the haycock, fast asleep.
Will you wake him? No, not I!
For if I do, he's sure to cry.

Theme Connections

Colors
Cows
Farms
Sheep

Little Fishes in a Brook

Little fishes in a brook,
Father caught them on a hook,
Mother fried them in a pan,
Johnnie eats them like a man.

Fishie, fishie in the brook,
Daddy catch him with a hook.
Mama fry him in a pan.
Baby eat him like a man.

Fishy, fishy in the brook,
Papa catch him with a hook,
Mama fry him for our sup,
Baby eat him all right up,
Yum, yum, yum, yum, yum, yum!

Theme Connections

Families
Fish
Food
Rivers

The Little Green Frog

Gunk, gunk went the little green frog one day.
Gunk, gunk went the little green frog.
Gunk, gunk went the little green frog one day.
And his eyes went ahh, ahh, gunk.
   (circle your fingers around your eyes and stick out your
   tongue)

Theme Connections

Animal Sounds
Colors
Frogs

Little Hunk of Tin
(Tune: I'm a Little Acorn Brown)

I'm a little hunk of tin.
(cup hand as if holding something)
Nobody knows what shape I'm in.
(hold hands to side palm up and shrug)
Got four wheels and a running board.
(hold up 4 fingers)
I'm a four-door.
(shake head yes)
I'm a Ford.

Chorus:
Honk, honk *(pull ear)*
Rattle, rattle. *(shake head)*
Crash, crash. *(push chin)*
Beep, beep. *(push nose)*
Repeat chorus twice.

Theme Connections

Sounds
Transportation

Little Jack Horner

Little Jack Horner sat in the corner.
Eating his Christmas pie.
He stuck in his thumb,
And pulled out a plum.
Then said, "What a good boy am I!"

Theme Connections

Food
Holidays
Self-esteem

Little King Pippin

Little King Pippin he built a fine hall,
Pie-crust and pastry-crust, that was the wall;
The windows were made of black pudding and white,
And slated with pancakes—you ne'er saw the like!

Variation

King Boggen, he built a fine new hall;
Pastry and piecrust, that was the wall;
The windows were made of black pudding and white,
Roofed with pancakes—you never saw the like.

Theme Connections

Food
Houses and Homes
Humor
Kings and Queens

Little Maid, Little Maid

Little maid, little maid, where have you been?
I've been to see grandmother over the green.
What did she give you?
Milk in a can.
What did you say for it?
Thank you, Grandam.

Theme Connection

Families

Little Miss Muffet

Little Miss Muffet sat on her tuffet,
Eating her curds and whey.
Along came a spider,
And sat down beside her,
And frightened Miss Muffet away.

Theme Connections

Emotions
Food
Spiders

Little Miss Tucket

Little Miss Tucket
Sat on a bucket,
Eating some peaches and cream.
There came a grasshopper
And tried hard to stop her,
But she said "Go away, or I'll scream."

Theme Connections

Emotions
Food
Grasshoppers

Little Mouse

Walk little mouse, walk little mouse. *(tiptoe around)*
Hide little mouse, hide little mouse. *(cover eyes with hands)*
Here comes the cat! *(look around)*
Run little mouse, run little mouse! *(walk quickly to the circle
  area and sit down)*

Theme Connections

Cats
Mice
Movement

Little Mousie

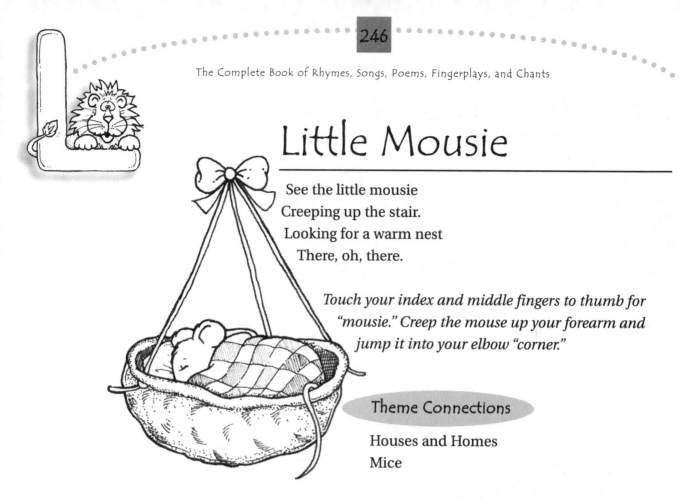

See the little mousie
Creeping up the stair.
Looking for a warm nest
There, oh, there.

Touch your index and middle fingers to thumb for "mousie." Creep the mouse up your forearm and jump it into your elbow "corner."

Theme Connections

Houses and Homes
Mice

Little Nancy Etticoat

Little Nancy Etticoat
In a white petticoat
And a red nose;
The longer she stands,
The shorter she grows.
(A candle)

Theme Connections

Colors
Humor

Little Poll Parrot

Little Poll Parrot
Sat in his garret,
Eating toast and tea;
A little brown mouse
Jumped into the house,
And stole it all away.

Theme Connections

Birds
Food
Mice

Little Red Apple

A little red apple grew high in a tree. *(point up)*
I looked up at it. *(shade eyes and look up)*
It looked down at me. *(shade eyes and look down)*
"Come down, please," I said. *(use hand to motion downward)*
And that little red apple fell right on my head. *(tap the top of your head)*

Theme Connections

Apples
Colors
Food
Seasons

Little Red Caboose

Little red caboose, chug, chug, chug.
Little red caboose, chug, chug, chug.
Little red caboose, behind the train, train, train, train.
Smokestack on his back, back, back, back.
Chugging down the track, track, track, track.
Little red caboose behind the train.

Theme Connections

Colors
Sounds of Language
Trains

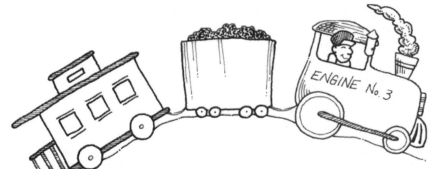

Little Red Wagon

(Tune: One Little, Two Little, Three Little Indians)

Bumpin' up and down in my little red wagon,
Bumpin' up and down in my little red wagon,
Bumpin' up and down in my little red wagon,
Havin' so much fun.

Here come my friends in their little red wagons,
Here come my friends in their little red wagons,
Here come my friends in their little red wagons,
Havin' so much fun.

Pull me around in my little red wagon,
Pull me around in my little red wagon,
Pull me around in my little red wagon,
Havin' so much fun.

Turn the corner in my little red wagon,
Turn the corner in my little red wagon,
Turn the corner in my little red wagon,
Havin' so much fun.

Bumpin' up and down in my little red wagon,
Bumpin' up and down in my little red wagon,
Bumpin' up and down in my little red wagon,
Havin' so much fun.

We're having so much fun!

Theme Connections

Colors   Toys
Friends   Transportation

Little Robin Red Breast

Little robin red breast, stay upon a rail.
(hold up thumb and little finger, and curl down rest of fingers)
Niddle, noodle went his head.
(wiggle thumb for head)
Wibble, wobble went his tail.
(wiggle baby finger for tail)

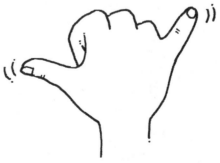

Theme Connections

Birds
Colors

Little Sir Echo

Little Sir Echo, how do you do?
Hello! (Hello!) Hello! (Hello!)
Little Sir Echo will answer you,
Hello! (Hello!) Hello! (Hello!)
Hello! (Hello!) Hello! (Hello!)
Oh, won't you come over and play? (and play?)
You're a dear little fellow,
I know by your voice,
But you're always so far away (away).

Theme Connections

Senses
Sounds of Language

Little Skunk's Hole
(Tune: Dixie)

Theme Connections

Humor
Skunks

Oh, I stuck my head
In the little skunk's hole,
And the little skunk said,
"Well, bless my soul!
Take it out! Take it out!
Take it out! Remove it!"

Oh, I didn't take it out,
And the little skunk said,
"If you don't take it out
You'll wish you had.
Take it out! Take it out!"
Pheew! I removed it!

Little Squirrel

I saw a little squirrel
Sitting in a tree;
He was eating a nut,
And wouldn't look at me.

Theme Connections

Nature
Squirrels

Little Tommy Tinker

Little Tommy Tinker *(sit down)*
Sat on a clinker*
And he began to cry,
"Oh Ma! *(stand up, throw hands high, then sit down again)*
Oh Ma!" *(stand up, throw hands high, then sit down again)*
Poor little innocent guy!

* A clinker is a piece of coal that is still hot.

Theme Connection

Emotions

Little Tommy Tittlemouse

Little Tommy Tittlemouse
Lived in a little house.
He caught fishes
In other men's ditches.

Theme Connections

Fish
Houses and Homes

Little Tommy Tucker

Little Tommy Tucker
Sings for his supper.
What shall he eat?
White bread and butter.
How shall he cut it
Without e'er a knife?
How will he be married
Without e'er a wife?

Theme Connections

Families
Food

Little White Rabbit

Little white rabbit,
Hop on one foot, one foot.
Little white rabbit,
Hop on two feet, two feet.
Little white rabbit,
Hop on three feet, three feet.
Little white rabbit,
Hop on no feet, no feet.

Theme Connections

Colors
Counting
Numbers
Parts of the Body
Rabbits

London Bridge

London Bridge is falling down,
Falling down, falling down.
London Bridge is falling down,
My fair lady.

Build it up with iron bars,
Iron bars, iron bars.
Build it up with iron bars,
My fair lady.

Iron bars will bend and break,
Bend and break, bend and break.
Iron bars will bend and break,
My fair lady.

Build it up with silver and gold,
Silver and gold, silver and gold.
Build it up with silver and gold,
My fair lady.

Take the key and lock her up
Lock her up, lock her up.
Take the key and lock her up,
My fair lady.

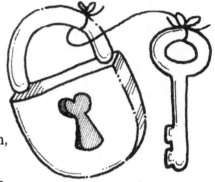

London Bridge is falling down,
Falling down, falling down.
London Bridge is falling down,
My fair lady.

Theme Connections

Colors
Movement

Looby Loo

Here we dance Looby-Loo,
Here we dance Looby-Light,
Here we dance Looby-Loo,
All on a Saturday night.

I put my right hand in,
I put my right hand out,
I give my hand a shake, shake, shake,
And turn myself about. Oh,

Chorus:
Here we dance Looby-Loo,
Here we dance Looby-Light,
Here we dance Looby-Loo,
All on a Saturday night.

I put my left hand in...
I put my right foot in...
I put my left foot in...
I put both hands in...
I put both feet in...
I put my head way in...
I put my whole self in...

Theme Connections

Days of the Week
Movement
Parts of the Body

Los Pollitos

Los pollitos dicen "pío, pío, pío,"
Cuando tienen hambre, *(toque el estómago)*
Cuando tienen frío. *(haga ademán de tener frío)*
La gallina busca el maíz y el trigo. *(con los manos, busque los granos)*
Les da la comida, *(toque la boca)*
Y les presta abrigo. *(póngalos debajo de los brazos para pro tegerlos)*
Acurrucaditos bajo las dos alas,
Hasta el otro día duermen los pollitos. *(haga ademán de dormir)*

English Translation

Baby chicks are singing "pío, pío, pío,"
"Mamma we are hungry. *(rub tummy)*
Mamma we are cold." *(cross arms over chest and shiver)*
Mamma looks for wheat. *(look around)*
Mamma looks for corn. *(pretend to pick something up)*
Mamma feeds them dinner. *(pretend to feed)*
Mamma keeps them warm. *(motion to come here)*

Under mamma's wings, sleeping in the hay, *(lift arm as if offering to hold)*
Baby chicks all huddle until the next day. *(place hands together and rest cheek on them)*

Theme Connections

Chickens
Families
Food
Languages

Lucy Locket

Lucy Locket lost her pocket,
Kitty Fisher found it.
Not a penny was there in it,
Only a ribbon 'round it.

Variation

Lucy Locket lost her pocket,
Kitty Fisher found it;
Nothing in it, nothing in it,
But the binding round it.

Theme Connections

Clothing
Money

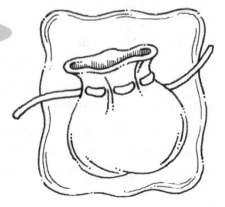

Make a Pancake

Make a pancake pat, pat, pat. *(pat hands together)*
Do not make it fat, fat, fat. *(stretch hands apart)*
You must make it flat, flat, flat. *(pat hands together)*
Make a pancake just like that. *(clap hands together)*

Theme Connections

Cooking
Food

Make New Friends/Amigos

Make new friends, but keep the old.
One is silver, the other's gold.

Haz nuevos amigos,
Pero retén los viejos.
Uno es plata, y el otro es oro.

Theme Connection

Friends

The Man in the Moon
(came down too soon)

The man in the moon
Came down too soon,
And asked his way to Norwich;
He went by the south,
And burnt his mouth
With supping cold plum porridge.

Theme Connections

Food
Humor
Naptime/Sleeping
Parts of the Body
Spatial Relationships
Sun, Moon, Stars

The Man in the Moon
(looked out of the moon)

The Man in the Moon looked out of the moon,
Looked out of the moon and said,
"Tis time for all children on the earth
To think about getting to bed!"

Variation

The man in the moon
Looked out of the moon,
And this is what he said,
"'Tis time that, now I'm getting up,
All babies went to bed."

Theme Connections

Families
Naptime/Sleeping
Sun, Moon, Stars

A Man in the Wilderness

A man in the wilderness
Asked this of me,
"How many strawberries
Grow in the sea?"
I answered him
As I thought good,
"As many red herrings
As swim in the wood."

Theme Connections

Colors
Humor

Mary Ann, Mary Ann

Mary Ann, Mary Ann
Make the porridge in a pan.
Make it thick, make it thin,
Make it any way you can.

Theme Connections

Cooking
Food

Mary Had a Little Lamb

Mary had a little lamb, little lamb, little lamb.
Mary had a little lamb,
Its fleece was white as snow.

Everywhere that Mary went, Mary went, Mary went,
Everywhere that Mary went,
The lamb was sure to go.

It followed her to school one day, school one day,
school one day.
It followed her to school one day,
Which was against the rules.

It made the children laugh and play, laugh and play, laugh
and play.
It made the children laugh and play,
To see a lamb at school.

And so the teacher turned it out, turned it out, turned it out.
And so the teacher turned it out,
But it lingered near.

And waited patiently about, patiently about, patiently
  about.
And waited patiently about,
'Till Mary did appear.

"Why does the lamb love Mary so? Mary so, Mary so."
"Why does the lamb love Mary so?"
The eager children cry.

"Why Mary loves the lamb, you know! Lamb you know,
  lamb you know!"
"Why Mary loves the lamb you know!"
The teacher did reply.

Theme Connections

School
Sheep

Mary, Mary

Mary, Mary, quite contrary,
How does your garden grow?
With silver bells and cockle shells,
And pretty maids all in a row.

Theme Connections

Flowers
Growing Things
Nature

Matthew, Mark, Luke and John

Matthew, Mark, Luke and John
Hold my horse 'till I leap on.
Hold him steady, hold him sure,
And I'll get over the misty moor.

Theme Connections

Horses

Me and You

I've got one head,
One nose too,
One mouth, one chin,
So have you.
I've got two eyes,
Two ears too,
Two arms, two legs,
And so have you.
I've got two hands,
Two thumbs too,
Four fingers on each hand,
And so have you.

Theme Connections

Parts of the Body
Self-esteem

Merry Are the Bells

Merry are the bells and merry would they ring.
Merry was myself and merry could I sing,
With a merry ding-dong.

Theme Connections

Music
Sounds of Language

Merry Ma Tanzie

Here we go round by jinga-ring,
Jinga ring, jinga ring.
Here we go round by jinga-ring
About the merry ma tanzie.

A lump of gold to tell her name,
Tell her name, tell her name.
A lump of gold to tell her name
About the merry ma tanzie.

Sweep the house till the bride comes home,
The bride comes home, the bride comes home.
Sweep the house till the bride comes home
About the merry ma tanzie.

Theme Connections

Families
Houses and Homes
Sounds of Language

Merry Sunshine

Good morning, merry sunshine!
How did you wake so soon?
You've scared the little stars away,
And shined away the moon.
I saw you go to sleep last night
Before I stopped my playing.
How did you get way over there,
And where have you been staying?

I never go to sleep, dear one,
I just go round to see
My little children of the
East who rise and watch for me.
I waken all the birds and bees
And flowers on my way.
And now come back to see the child
Who stayed out late to play.

Theme Connections

Nature
Sun, Moon, Stars
Time of Day

Michael Finnegan

There was an old man named Michael Finnegan.
He had whiskers on his chinnegan.
They fell out and then grew in again.
Poor old Michael Finnegan,
Begin again.

There was an old man named Michael Finnegan.
He went fishing with a pin again.
Caught a fish and dropped it in again.
Poor old Michael Finnegan,
Begin again.

There was an old man named Michael Finnegan.
He grew fat and then grew thin again.
Then he died and had to begin again.
Poor old Michael Finnegan,
Begin again.

Variation

I know a man named Michael Finnegan.
He wears whiskers on his chinnegan.
Along came a wind and blew them in again.
Poor old Michael Finnegan, begin again.

Theme Connections

Fish
Humor
Opposites

Michael, Row the Boat Ashore

Michael, row the boat ashore,
Hallelujah.
Michael, row the boat ashore,
Hallelujah.

Sister, help to trim the sails,
Hallelujah.
Sister, help to trim the sails,
Hallelujah.

River Jordan's deep and wide,
Hallelujah.
Milk and honey on the other side,
Hallelujah.

River Jordan's chilly and cold,
Hallelujah.
Chills the body, but warms the soul,
Hallelujah.

Theme Connections

Boats and Ships
Families
Rivers

Milkman, Milkman

Milkman, milkman, where have you been?
In Buttermilk channel up to my chin.
I spilt my milk and I spoilt my clothes,
And I got a long icicle hung from my nose.

Theme Connections

Occupations
Weather
Work

Miss Mary Mack

Miss Mary Mack, Mack, Mack
All dressed in black, black, black
With silver buttons, buttons, buttons
All down her back, back, back.
She asked her mother, mother, mother
For fifteen cents, cents, cents
To see the elephants, elephants, elephants
Jump the fence, fence, fence.
They jumped so high, high, high
They touched the sky, sky, sky,
And they didn't come back, back, back
Till the fourth of July, ly, ly.

And they didn't come down, down, down
Till the fourth of July.

Theme Connections

Colors	Holidays	Money
Elephants	Humor	

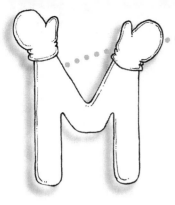

Miss Polly Had a Dolly

Miss Polly had a dolly
Who was sick, sick, sick,
So she called for the doctor
To be quick, quick, quick;
The doctor came
With his bag and his hat,
And he knocked at the door
With a rat-a-tat-tat.

He looked at the dolly
And he shook his head,
And he said, "Miss Polly,
Put her straight to bed."
He wrote out a paper
For a pill, pill, pill,
"That'll make her better,
Yes it will, will, will!"

Variation

He wrote out a paper
For a pill, pill, pill,
"I'll be back in the morning
With the bill, bill, bill."

Theme Connections

Humor
Occupations

Mister Sun

Oh, Mister Sun, Sun, Mister Golden Sun
Won't you please shine down on me?
Oh, Mister Sun, Sun, Mister Golden Sun
Hiding behind that tree.
These little children are asking you
To please come out so we can play with you.
Oh, Mister Sun, Sun, Mister Golden Sun,
Won't you please shine down on me?

Theme Connections

Sun, Moon, Stars

Monday's Child

Monday's child is fair of face.
Tuesday's child is full of grace.
Wednesday's child is full of woe.
Thursday's child has far to go.
Friday's child is loving and giving.
Saturday's child works hard for a living.
But the child who is born on Sunday
Is fair and wise and good and gay.

Theme Connections

Days of the Week
Emotions

The Moon Shines Bright

The moon shines bright,
The stars give a light.
You may play at any game
At ten o'clock at night.

Theme Connections

Sun, Moon, Stars
Time of Day

The More We Get Together

The more we get together,
Together, together.
The more we get together,
The happier we'll be.

For your friends are my friends,
And my friends are your friends.
The more we get together,
The happier we'll be.

Theme Connections

Emotions
Friends
Self-esteem

Moses Supposes

Moses supposes his toeses are roses,
But Moses supposes erroneously;
For nobody's toeses are posies of roses
As Moses supposes his toeses to be.

Theme Connections

Humor
Parts of the Body

Mother, May I

Mother, may I go out to swim?
Yes, my darling daughter.
Hang your clothes on a hickory limb,
But don't go near the water.

Theme Connections

Clothing
Families
Humor

Mr. Nobody

I know a funny little man,
As quiet as a mouse,
Who does the mischief that is done
In everybody's house!

There's no one ever sees his face,
And yet we all agree
That every plate we break was cracked
By Mr. Nobody.

'Tis he who always tears our books,
Who leaves the door ajar.
He pulls the buttons from our
shirts,
And scatters pins afar.

That squeaking door will always squeak,
For, prithee, don't you see,
We leave the oiling to be done
By Mr. Nobody.

He puts damp wood upon the fire,
That kettles cannot boil;
His are the feet that bring in mud,
And all the carpets soil.

The finger marks upon the door
By none of us are made;
We never leave the blinds unclosed,
To let the curtains fade.

The ink we never spill; the boots
That lying round you see
Are not our boots; — they all belong
To Mr. Nobody.

Theme Connections

Families
Houses and Homes
Humor

Mr. Turkey

Mr. Turkey's tail is big and wide. *(spread hands wide)*
He swings it when he walks. *(swing hands back and forth)*
His neck is long, his chin is red. *(stroke chin and neck)*
He gobbles when he talks. *(open and close hand)*

Mr. Turkey is so tall and proud. *(stand up tall)*
He dances on his feet. *(dance in place)*
And on each Thanksgiving Day,
He's something good to eat. *(pat stomach)*

Theme Connections

Holidays
Parts of the Body
Turkeys

Muffin Man

Oh, do you know the muffin man,
The muffin man, the muffin man?
Oh, do you know the muffin man
Who lives on Drury Lane?

Oh, yes I know the muffin man,
The muffin man, the muffin man.
Oh, yes I know the muffin man
Who lives on Drury Lane.

Theme Connections

Food
Neighborhoods

The Mulberry Bush

Here we go 'round the mulberry bush, *(hold hands and walk in circle)*
The mulberry bush, the mulberry bush.
Here we go 'round the mulberry bush
So early in the morning.

This is the way we wash our clothes, *(suit actions to words)*
Wash our clothes, wash our clothes.
This is the way we wash our clothes
So early Monday morning.

This is the way we iron our clothes…Tuesday morning.
This is the way we scrub the floors…Wednesday morning.
This is the way we sew our clothes…Thursday morning.
This is the way we sweep the house…Friday morning.
This is the way we bake our bread…Saturday morning.
This is the way we go to church…Sunday morning.

Variation

End each verse with "On a cold and frosty morning" instead of "So early in the morning." There is also a variant verse (which, as a mother, I appreciate), which goes "This is the way we clean our rooms, clean our rooms, clean our rooms…"

Theme Connections

Clothing
Cooking
Days of the Week
Houses and Homes
Work

My Apple

Look at my apple, it is nice and round. *(cup hands)*
It fell from a tree, down to the ground. *(move fingers in a downward motion)*
Come, let me share my apple, please do! *(beckoning motion)*
My mother can cut it half in two— *(slicing motion)*
One half for me and one half for you. *(hold out two hands, sharing halves)*

Theme Connections

Apples
Friends
Shapes

My Big Balloon

I can make a big balloon,
Watch me while I blow.
Small at first, then bigger,
Watch it grow and grow.

Do you think it's big enough?
Maybe I should stop.
For if I blow much longer,
My balloon will surely pop!

Theme Connection

Opposites

My Bike

One wheel, two wheels *(make circles with arms)*
On the ground,
My feet make the pedals *(lift feet and pretend to pedal bike)*
Go round and round.
The handlebars help me *(pretend to steer)*
Steer so straight,
Down the sidewalk *(shade eyes as if looking at something
     in the distance)*
     And through the gate.

Theme Connections

Counting
Movement
Numbers
Self-esteem

My Bonnie Lies Over the Ocean

My Bonnie lies over the ocean,
My Bonnie lies over the sea.
My Bonnie lies over the ocean,
Please bring back my Bonnie to me.

Chorus:
Bring back,
Bring back,
Oh, bring back my Bonnie to me, to me.
Bring back,
Bring back,
Oh, bring back my Bonnie to me.

Oh, blow ye winds o'er the ocean,
And blow ye winds o'er the sea.
Oh, blow ye winds o'er the ocean,
And bring back my Bonnie to me.

Chorus

The winds have blown over the ocean.
The winds have blown over the sea.
The winds have blown over the ocean,
And brought back my Bonnie to me.

Chorus

Theme Connections

Boats and Ships
Emotions
Families
Oceans and Seas
Weather
Wind

My Dog Rags

I have a dog and his name is Rags, *(point to self)*
He eats so much that his tummy sags, *(put hands
    together in front of stomach)*
His ears flip flop and his tail wig wags, *(bend each
    hand at wrist)*
And when he walks he zig, zig, zags! *(make an imaginary
    "Z" with index finger)*

Theme Connections

Dogs   Humor

My Eyes Can See

(suit actions to words)
My eyes can see.
My mouth can talk.
My ears can hear.
My feet can walk.

My nose can sniff.
My teeth can chew.
My lids can flutter.
My arms hug you.

Theme Connections

Emotions
Parts of the Body
Self-esteem

My Father Is Extremely Tall

My father is extremely tall
   When he stands upright like a wall—
    But I am very short and small.
   Yet I am growing, so they say,
A little taller every day.

Theme Connections

Families
Growing Up
Opposites

My Father Owns a Butcher Shop

My father owns a butcher shop,
My mother cuts the meat,
And I'm the little hot dog
That runs around the street.

Theme Connections

Food
Occupations

My Favorite Toys

I have a lot of favorite toys.
I cannot choose just one.
I need to keep them all around
For different kinds of fun.

A book, a doll,
  A drum, a ball,
    And, of course, my teddy bear.
    A wagon, a trike,
  And finally I like
The jack-in-the-box sitting there.

As you can see, I need them all
For work and play and rest.
When you go home to find your toys,
Which ones do you like best?

Theme Connections

Teddy Bears
Toys

My Grandfather's Clock

My grandfather's clock
Was too large for the shelf,
So it stood ninety years on the floor;
It was taller by half
Than the old man himself,
Though it weighed not a pennyweight more.
It was bought on the morn

Of the day that he was born,
And was always his treasure and pride;

Chorus:
But it stopped short
Never to go again,
When the old man died.
Ninety years without slumbering,
Tick, tock, tick, tock,
His life seconds numbering,
Tick, tock, tick, tock,
It stopped short
Never to go again,
When the old man died.

In watching its pendulum
Swing to and fro,
Many hours had he spent while a boy;
And in childhood and manhood
The clock seemed to know,
And to share both his grief and his joy.
For it struck twenty-four
When he entered at the door,
With a blooming and beautiful bride;

Chorus

My grandfather said
That of those he could hire,
Not a servant so faithful he found;
For it wasted no time,
And had but one desire,
At the close of each week to be wound.
And it kept in its place,
Not a frown upon its face,
And its hand never hung by its side.

Chorus

It rang an alarm
In the dead of the night,
An alarm that for years had been dumb;
And we knew that his spirit
Was pluming his flight,
That his hour of departure had come.
Still the clock kept the time,
With a soft and muffled chime,
As we silently stood by his side.

Chorus

Theme Connections

Emotions
Families
Time of Day

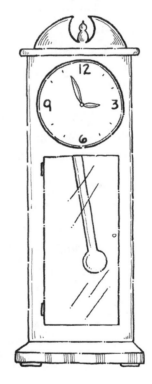

My Hand on Myself

My hand on my head, *(place hand on head)*
What have I here? *(open arms palm up)*
This is my topnotcher, *(point to head)*
Mamma, my dear.
Topnotcher, topnotcher, *(point to head again)*
Dickie, dickie, doo *(knock on head)*
That's what I learned in school. *(shake index finger)*
Boom! Boom!

My hand on my brow, *(place hand on brow)*
What have I here? *(open arms palm up)*
This is my sweat boxer, *(point to forehead)*
Mamma, my dear.
Sweat boxer, topnotcher, *(point to head and then forehead)*
Dickie, dickie, doo *(knock on head)*
That's what I learned in school. *(shake index finger)*
Boom! Boom!

(continue adding body parts and suit hand motions to words)
Eye—eye blinker
Nose—nose blower
Mouth—food grinder
Chin—chin chopper
Heart—chest ticker
Stomach—bread basket
Knees—knee benders
Toes—pedal pushers

Theme Connections

Humor
Parts of the Body
School

My Hat, It Has Three Corners

My hat, it has three corners,
Three corners has my hat;
And had it not three corners,
It would not be my hat.

_____ hat, it has three corners,
Three corners has _____ hat;
And had it not three corners,
It would not be _____ hat.

_____ _____, it has three corners,
Three corners has _____ _____;
And had it not three corners,
It would not be _____ _____.
_____ _____, it has _____ corners,
_____ corners has _____ _____
And had it not _____ corners,
It would not be _____ _____.
_____ _____, it has _____ _____,
_____ _____ has _____ _____
And had it not _____ _____,
It would not be _____ _____.

Theme Connections

Hats
Movement
Numbers

Actions:
My—Point to self
Hat—Point to head
Three—Hold up three fingers
Corners—Bend arm and point to elbow
Omit the words in verses where "_____" is displayed, but do
the corresponding actions.

My Head

(suit actions to words)
This is the circle that is my head.
This is my mouth with which words are said.
These are my eyes with which I see.
This is my nose that is part of me.
This is the hair that grows on my head,
And this is my hat I wear on my head.

Theme Connections

Clothing
Parts of the Body
Shapes

My Little Sister

My little sister dressed in pink
Washed all the dishes in the sink.
How many dishes did she break?
One, two, three, four, five.

Theme Connections

Colors
Counting
Families
Numbers
Work

My Mama Told Me

My mama told me to tell you
To clap your hands
Just like I do. *(clap hands)*
My mama told me to tell you
To shake your head
Just like I do. *(shake head)*

Theme Connections

Families
Parts of the Body

Continue with:

Tap your toes…
Bend your knees…
Throw a kiss…

My Old Hen's a Good Old Hen

My old hen's a good old hen.
She lays eggs for sailor men.
Sometimes one, sometimes two.
Sometimes enough for the whole blamed crew.

Theme Connections

Chickens
Numbers

My Shadow
by Robert Louis Stevenson

I have a little shadow that goes in and out with me,
And what can be the use of him is more than I can see.
He is very, very like me from the heels up to the head;
And I see him jump before me, when I jump into my bed.

The funniest thing about him is the way he likes to grow.
Not at all like proper children, which is always very slow;
For he sometimes shoots up taller like an india-rubber ball,
And he sometimes gets so little that there's none of him at all.

Theme Connections

Movement
Self-esteem

North Wind Doth Blow

The north wind doth blow,
And we shall have snow.
And what will the robin do then, poor thing?
He will sit in the barn and keep himself warm,
With his little head tucked under his wing, poor thing!

Theme Connections

Birds
Farms
Seasons
Weather

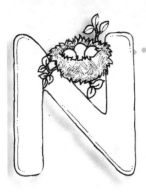

Nose, Nose, Jolly Red Nose

Nose, nose, jolly red nose,
And who gave thee that jolly red nose?
Nutmeg and ginger, cinnamon and cloves,
That's what gave me this jolly red nose.

Theme Connections

Colors
Cooking

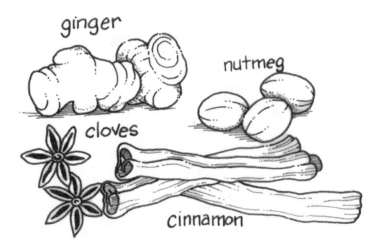

Now We Are Gathering Nuts in May

Now we are gathering nuts in May
Nuts in May, nuts in May.
Now we are gathering nuts in May
Out on a frosty morning.

Who will come over for nuts in May
Nuts in may, nuts in May.
Who will come over for nuts in May
Out on a frosty morning?

Sue will come over for nuts in May
Nuts in May, nuts in May.
Sue will come over for nuts in May
Out on a frosty morning.

Who will come over to fetch her away
Fetch her away, fetch her away.
Who will come over to fetch her away
Out on a frosty morning?

Jack will come over to fetch her away
Fetch her away, fetch her away.
Jack will come over to fetch her away
Out on a frosty morning.

Theme Connections

Seasons
Time of Day

Nut Tree

I had a little nut tree.
Nothing would it bear
But a silver nutmeg
And a golden pear.

The King of Spain's daughter
Came to visit me,
And all for the sake
Of my little nut tree.

Variation

I had a little nut tree, nothing would it bear
But a silver nutmeg and a golden pear.
The King of Spain's daughter came to visit me,
And all for the sake of my little nut tree.
I skipped over water, I danced over sea,
And all the birds in the air couldn't catch me.

Theme Connections

Growing Things
Kings and Queens
Nature

Oats, Peas, Beans, and Barley Grow

(suit actions to words)
Oats, peas, beans, and barley grow,
Oats, peas, beans, and barley grow,
Neither you nor I nor anyone
knows
How oats, peas, beans, and barley grow.

First the farmer sows his seed,
Then he stands and takes his ease,
Stamps his feet and claps his hands,
And turns around and sees the land.

Waiting for a partner.
Waiting for a partner.
Open the ring and bring one in,
And now we'll gaily dance and sing.

Theme Connections

Farms
Growing Things

Oh, Dear, What Can the Matter Be?

Oh, dear, what can the matter be?
Dear, dear, what can the matter be?
Oh, dear, what can the matter be?
Johnny's so long at the fair.

He promised to buy me a bunch of blue ribbons;
He promised to buy me some bonny blue ribbons;
He promised to buy me a bunch of blue ribbons,
To bind up my bonny brown hair.

And it's, oh, dear what can the matter be?
Dear, dear, what can the matter be?
Oh, dear, what can the matter be?
Johnny's so long at the fair.

Theme Connections

Colors
Emotions
Friends

Oh, How Lovely Is the Evening

Theme Connections

Sounds of Language
Time of Day

Oh, how lovely is the evening, is the evening,
When the bells are sweetly ringing, sweetly ringing.
Ding, dong, ding! Ding, dong, ding!

Oh, the Mighty King of France

Oh, the mighty king of France,
He marched his men to war.
But none of them got to the battlefield
Because it was too far.

Theme Connections

Humor
Kings and Queens

Oh, Rare Harry Parry

Oh, rare Harry Parry
When will you marry?
When apples and pears are ripe,
I'll come to your wedding
Without any bidding,
And dance and sing all night.

Theme Connections

Celebrations
Emotions
Fall

Oh, You Can't Get to Heaven

Verse 1: Oh, you can't get to heaven
(Oh, you can't get to heaven)
On roller skates.
(On roller skates)
'Cause you'd roll right by
('Cause you'd roll right by)
Those pearly gates.
(Those pearly gates)

Oh you can't get to heaven on roller skates
'Cause you'd roll right by those pearly gates.
I ain't gonna grieve my Lord no more.

Theme Connections

Humor

Chorus: I ain't gonna grieve my Lord no more.
I ain't gonna grieve my Lord no more.
I ain't gonna grieve my Lord no more.

Verse 2: Oh, you can't get to heaven
(Oh, you can't get to heaven)
In a rocking chair
(In a rocking chair)
'Cause a rocking chair
('Cause a rocking chair)
Won't get you there
(Won't get you there)

Oh, you can't get to heaven in a rocking chair
'Cause a rocking chair won't get you there.
I ain't gonna grieve my Lord no more.

Chorus

Old Dan Tucker

Old Dan Tucker went to town
Riding a goat and leading a hound.
The hound gave a yelp and the goat gave a jump
And old Dan Tucker landed on a stump.

Theme Connections

Dogs
Goats
Humor

Old Gray Cat

The old gray cat is sleeping, sleeping, sleeping.
The old gray cat is sleeping in the house. *(one child, the cat, curls up, pretending to sleep)*

The little mice are creeping, creeping, creeping.
The little mice are creeping through the house. *(other children, the mice, creep around the cat)*

Theme Connections

Cats
Houses and Homes
Mice
Movement

The old gray cat is waking, waking, waking.
The old gray cat is waking in the house. *(cat slowly sits up and stretches)*

The old gray cat is chasing, chasing, chasing.
The old gray cat is chasing through the house. *(cat chases mice)*

All the mice are squealing, squealing, squealing.
All the mice are squealing through the house. *(mice squeal; when cat catches a mouse, that mouse becomes the cat)*

Old Gray Mare

The old gray mare, she
Ain't what she used to be,
Ain't what she used to be,
Ain't what she used to be.
The old gray mare, she
Ain't what she used to be,
Many long years ago,
Many long years ago,
Many long years ago.
The old gray mare, she
Ain't what she used to be,
Many long years ago.

Theme Connections

Horses

Old King Cole

Old King Cole was a merry old soul,
And a merry old soul was he.
He called for his pipe
And he called for his bowl,
And he called for his fiddlers three.
Each fiddler he had a fiddle,
And the fiddles went tweedle-dee.
Oh, there's none so rare as can compare
As King Cole and his fiddlers three.

Then he called for his fifers two,
And they puffed and they blew tootle-too.
And King Cole laughed as his glass he quaffed,
And his fifers puffed tootle-too.

Then he called for his drummer boy,
The army's pride and joy.
And the thuds rang out with a loud bang, bang,
The noise of the noisiest toy.

Then he called for his trumpeters four,
Who stood at his own palace door.
And they played trang-a-tang
Whilst the drummer went bang,
And King Cole he called for more.

He called for a man to conduct,
Who into his bed had been tucked,
And he had to get up without bite or sup,
And waggle his stick and conduct.

Old King Cole laughed with glee,
Such rare antics to see.
There never was a man in merry England
Who was half as merry as he.

Theme Connections

Kings and Queens
Music
Numbers
Sounds of Language

Old MacDonald Had a Farm

Old MacDonald had a farm, E-I-E-I-O
   And on this farm she had a cow, E-I-E-I-O
   With a moo, moo here,
   And a moo, moo there,
   Here a moo, there a moo,
   Everywhere a moo, moo.
   Old MacDonald had a farm, E-I-E-I-O!

Additional verses:
   Pig—oink, oink
   Cat—meow, meow
   Dog—bow-wow
   Horse—neigh, neigh

Theme Connections

Cats	Farms	Sounds
Cows	Horses	
Dogs	Pigs	

Old Mother Goose

Old Mother Goose,
When she wanted to wander,
Would ride through the air
On a very fine gander.

Theme Connections

Geese

Old Mother Hubbard

Old Mother Hubbard
Went to the cupboard
To get her poor dog a bone
But when she came there
The cupboard was bare,
And so the poor dog had none.

She went to the hatter's
To buy him a hat,
But when she came back
He was feeding the cat.

She went to the grocer's
To buy him some fruit,
But when she came back
He was playing the flute.

She went to the tailor's
To buy him a coat,
But when she came back
He was riding the goat.

She went to the barber's
To buy him a wig,
But when she came back
He was dancing a jig.

She went to the cobbler's
To buy him some shoes,
But when she came back
He was reading the news.

Theme Connections

Cats	Goats
Dogs	Humor
Food	Occupations

The Old Woman

The old woman must stand at the tub, tub, tub.
The dirty clothes to rub, rub, rub.
But when they are clean and fit to be seen,
She'll dress like a lady and dance on the green.

Theme Connections

Clothing	Movement

The Old Woman's Pie

There was an old woman,
As I have heard tell,
She went to sell pie,
But her pie would not sell.

She hurried back home,
But her doorstep was high,
She stumbled and fell,
And a dog ate her pie.

Theme Connections

Dogs
Food

Oliver Twist
(can you do this?)

Oliver Twist, can you do this?
If so, do so.
Number one, touch your tongue.
Number two, touch your shoe.
Number three, touch your knees.
Number four, touch the floor.
Number five, jump up high.

Theme Connections

Counting
Movement
Numbers
Parts of the Body

Oliver Twist
(couldn't do this)

Oliver Twist couldn't do this.
What's the use of trying so?
Give him my toe. Over you go.
Oliver, Oliver Twisteo.

Theme Connections

Movement
Parts of the Body

On a Dark, Dark Night

On a dark, dark night,
In the dark, dark woods,
In a dark, dark house,
In a dark, dark room,
In a dark, dark cupboard,
In a dark, dark box,
There's a GHOST!

*Use scary whisper until the word GHOST. This is
often done with one person saying a line, and everyone repeating it in a ghostly voice.*

Theme Connections

Holidays
Time of Day

On Saturday Night

On Saturday night I lost my wife,
And where do you think I found her?
Up in the moon, singing a tune,
And all the stars around her.

Theme Connections

Days of the Week
Sun, Moon, Stars
Time of Day

Once I Saw a Little Bird

Once I saw a little bird
Come hop, hop, hop.
And I cried, "Little bird,
Will you stop, stop, stop?"
I was going to the window
To say, "How do you do?"
When he shook his little tail,
And away he flew.

Theme Connections

Birds
Movement

One Dark and Stormy Night

Late one dark and stormy night, *(use spooky voice)*
Three little witches are stirring a pot. *(stir imaginary pot)*
Two little ghosts say, "How d' ye do?" *(lower voice gradually)*
Go tiptoe, tiptoe, tiptoe. *(barely whisper)*
Booooo! *(very loud)*

Theme Connections

Counting
Holidays
Nighttime
Numbers

One Elephant

One elephant went out to play
On a spider's web one day.
He had such enormous fun,
He asked another elephant to come.

Two elephants went out to play...
Three elephants went out to play...
Four elephants went out to play...
Five elephants went out to play...

Theme Connections

Elephants
Humor

One Finger, One Thumb, Keep Moving

(suit actions to words)
One finger, one thumb, keep moving,
One finger, one thumb, keep moving,
One finger, one thumb, keep moving,
We'll all be merry and bright.

One finger, one thumb, one arm, keep moving…
One finger, one thumb, one arm, one leg, keep moving…
One finger, one thumb, one arm, one leg, one nod of the
   head, keep moving…
One finger, one thumb, one arm, one leg, one nod of the
   head, stand up, sit down, keep moving…
One finger, one thumb, one arm, one leg, one nod of the
   head, stand up, turn round, sit down, keep moving…

Theme Connections

Humor
Movement
Parts of the Body

One for the Money

One for the money,
Two for the show,
Three to make ready,
And four to go!

Theme Connections

Counting   Numbers

One for the Mouse

One for the mouse,
One for the crow,
One to rot,
One to grow.

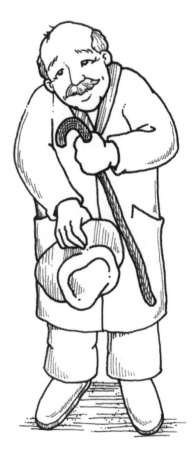

Theme Connections

Counting
Growing Things
Numbers

One Misty, Moisty Morning

One misty, moisty morning,
When cloudy was the weather,
I chanced to meet an old man
Clothed all in leather.
He began to compliment,
And I began to grin,
How do you do,
And how do you do,
And how do you do, again?

Theme Connections

Time of Day
Weather

One Old Oxford Ox

One old Oxford ox opening oysters.
Two toads totally tired trying to trot to Tisbury.
Three thick thumping tigers taking toast for tea.
Four finicky fishermen fishing for funny fish.
Five frippery Frenchmen foolishly fishing for frogs.
Six sportsmen shooting snipe.
Seven Severn salmon swallowing shrimp.
Eight eminent Englishmen eagerly examining Europe.
Nine nibbling noblemen nibbling nectarines.
Ten tinkering tinkers tinkering ten tin tinderboxes.
Eleven elephants elegantly equipped.
Twelve typographical topographers typically
    translating types.

Theme Connections

Counting
Numbers
Sound of Language

One Potato, Two Potato

One potato, two potato, *(make two fists, alternate tapping*
  one on top of the other)
Three potato, four,
Five potato, six potato,
Seven potato, more.
Eight potato, nine potato,
Where is ten?
Now we must count over again.

Theme Connections

Counting
Food
Numbers

One to Make Ready

One to make ready,
Two to prepare,
Good luck to the rider,
And away goes the mare!

Theme Connections

Counting
Horses
Numbers

One, Two

One, two,
Buckle my shoe;
Three, four,
Shut the door;
Five, six,
Pick up sticks;
Seven, eight,
Lay them straight;
Nine, ten,
A good fat hen;
Eleven, twelve,
Who will delve?
Thirteen, fourteen,
Maids a-courting;
Fifteen, sixteen,
Maids in the kitchen.
Seventeen, eighteen,
Maids in waiting,
Nineteen, twenty,
My plate's empty.

Variation

1,2, Tie my shoe.
3,4, Shut the door.
5,6, Pick up sticks.
7,8, Lay them straight.
9, 10, A big fat hen.
Let's get up and count again!

Theme Connections

Counting
Numbers

One, Two, Three, Four

One, two, three, four
Mary at the cottage door.
Five, six, seven, eight
Eating cherries off a plate.

Theme Connections

Counting
Food
Houses and Homes
Numbers

One, Two, Three, Four, Five

One, two, three, four, five,
Once I caught a fish alive.
Six, seven, eight, nine, ten,
Then I let it go again.
Why did you let it go?
Because it bit my finger so.
Which finger did it bite?
The little one upon the right.

Variation

One two, three, four, five
Once I caught a fish alive.
Why did you let it go?
Because it bit my finger so.
Six, seven, eight, nine, ten
Shall we go to fish again?
Not today, some other time
For I have broke my fishing line.

Theme Connections

Counting
Fish
Numbers

One's None

One's none.
Two's some.
Three's many.
Four's a penny.
Five's a little hundred.

Theme Connections

Counting
Numbers

Open, Shut Them
(Ábranlas, ciérrenlas)

(suit hand motions to words)
Open, shut them.
Open, shut them.
Give a little clap. *(clap)*
Open, shut them.
Open, shut them.
Put them in your lap.

Creep them, creep them, *(walk fingers up chest to chin)*
Creep them, creep them.
Right up to your chin.
Open up your little mouth, *(open mouth)*
But do not let them in.

Falling, falling,
Falling, falling
Right down to the ground. *(touch the ground with fingers)*
Then you pick them up again, *(bring hands back to lap)*
And turn them round and round.

Faster, faster
Faster, faster
Give a little clap. *(clap faster)*
Slower, slower
Slower, slower
Place them in your lap. *(place hands in lap)*

Spanish Translation

Ábranlas, ciérrenlas
Ábranlas, ciérrenlas, ábranlas, ciérrenlas,
Damé un aplauso.
Ábranlas, ciérrenlas, ábranlas, ciérrenlas,
Ponganlas acá.

Falling, falling slowly downward,
Nearly to the ground;
Quickly raise them, all the fingers,
Twirling round and round.

Variation

Open, shut them
Give a little clap
Open, shut them
Open shut them,
Lay them in your lap.

Roll them, roll them, roll them, roll them.
Give a little clap.
Roll them, roll them, roll them, roll them;
Lay them in your lap.

Creep them, creep them, slowly upward
To the rosy cheek;
Open wide the shining eyes;
Through the fingers peek.

Open, shut them, open, shut them,
To the shoulders fly;
Let them like the birdies flutter,
Flutter to the sky.

Theme Connections

Movement
Parts of the Body
Self-esteem

O, Susanna

Oh, I've come from Alabama
With my banjo on my knee,
I'm goin' to Louisiana
My true love for to see;
It rained all night the day I left,
The weather it was dry;
The sun so hot I froze to death;
Susanna, don't you cry.

Chorus: O, Susanna,
O, don't you cry for me,
I've come from Alabama
With my banjo on my knee.
O, Susanna, O, don't you cry for me,
'Cause I'm goin' to Louisiana,
My true love for to see.

I had a dream the other night
When ev'rything was still;
I thought I saw Susanna
A-comin' down the hill,
The buckwheat cake was in her mouth,
The tear was in her eye;
Says I, I'm comin' from the south,
Susanna, don't you cry.

Chorus

I soon will be in New Orleans,
And then I'll look around,
And when I find Susanna
I'll fall upon the ground.
And if I do not find her,
Then I will surely die,
And when I'm dead and buried,
Susanna, don't you cry.

Theme Connections

Emotions
Music

Over in the Meadow

Over in the meadow, in the sand, in the sun,
Lived an old mother frog and her little froggie one.
"Croak!" said the mother; "I croak!" said the one,
So they croaked and they croaked in the sand, in the sun.

Over in the meadow, in the stream so blue,
Lived an old mother fish and her little fishies two.
"Swim!" said the mother; "We swim!" said the two.
So they swam and they swam in the stream so blue.

Over in the meadow, on a branch of the tree,
Lived an old mother bird and her little birdies three.
"Sing!" said the mother; "We sing!" said the three,
And they sang and they sang on a branch of the tree.

Theme Connections

Animal sounds
Birds
Counting
Families
Fish
Frogs
Nature

Over the River and Through the Wood

Over the river and through the wood,
To grandfather's house we go;
The horse knows the way
To carry the sleigh,
Through the white and drifted snow, oh!

Over the river and through the wood,
Oh, how the wind does blow!
It stings the toes,
And bites the nose,
As over the ground we go.

Over the river and through the wood,
To have a first-rate play;
Oh, hear the bell ring,
"Ting-a-ling-ling!" Hurrah for
Thanksgiving Day-ay!

Over the river and through the wood,
Trot fast my dapple gray!
Spring over the ground,
Like a hunting hound!
For this is Thanksgiving Day.

Theme Connections

Celebrations
Holidays
Horses
Weather

The Owl and the Pussycat

by Edward Lear

The owl and the pussycat went to sea
In a beautiful pea-green boat
They took some honey and plenty of money
Wrapped up in a five-pound note.

The owl looked up to the stars above
And sang to a small guitar,
"O, lovely pussy, o pussy my love,
What a beautiful pussy you are, you are
What a beautiful pussy you are!"

Pussy said to the owl, "You elegant fowl,
How charmingly sweet you sing.
O, let us be married, too long we have tarried,
But what shall we do for a ring?"

They sailed away for a year and a day
To the land where the Bongtree grows.
And there in a wood a Piggywig stood
With a ring at the end of his nose, his nose,
With a ring at the end of his nose.

"Dear Pig, are you willing to sell for one shilling
Your ring?" Said the Piggy, "I will."
So they took it away and were married next day
By the turkey who lives on the hill.

They dined on mince and slices of quince
Which they ate with a runcible spoon;
And hand in hand on the edge of the sand
They danced by the light of the moon, the moon,
They danced by the light of the moon.

Theme Connections

Boats and Ships
Cats
Emotions
Owls
Pigs
Sun, Moon, and Stars

Pat-a-Cake

Pat-a-cake, pat-a-cake, baker's man. *(clap hands together)*
Bake me a cake as fast as you can.
Roll it, *(roll hands over each other)*
And pat it, *(pat hands together)*
And mark it with B, *(draw B in the air)*
And put it in the oven for baby and me. *(touch tummy)*

Theme Connections

Babies
Cooking
Food

Pawpaw Patch

Where, oh where,
Is dear little Nellie?
Where, oh where,
Is dear little Nellie?
Where, oh where,
Is dear little Nellie?
Way down yonder
In the pawpaw* patch.

Come on, boys,
Let's go find her.
Come on, boys,
Let's go find her,
Come on, boys,
Let's go find her,
Way down yonder
In the pawpaw patch.

Picking up pawpaws,
Puttin' 'em in your pocket,
Picking up pawpaws,
Puttin' 'em in your pocket,
Picking up pawpaws,
Puttin' 'em in your pocket,
Way down yonder
In the pawpaw patch.

Theme Connections

Clothing
Friends

* Pawpaws grow on trees in the central and southern
United States. The fruit is oblong and yellowish, and is
related to the papaya.

Peanut Butter

Chorus:
Peanut, peanut butter—jelly!
Peanut, peanut butter—jelly!

First you take the peanuts and *(pretend to dig peanuts)*
You dig 'em, you dig 'em.
Dig 'em, dig 'em, dig 'em.
Then you smash 'em, you smash 'em. *(pretend to smash peanuts)*
Smash 'em, smash 'em, smash 'em.
Then you spread 'em, you spread 'em. *(pretend to spread the peanuts)*
Spread 'em, spread 'em, spread 'em.

Chorus

Then you take the berries and *(pretend to pick berries)*
You pick 'em, you pick 'em.
Pick 'em, pick 'em, pick 'em.
Then you smash 'em, you smash 'em. *(pretend to smash berries)*
Smash 'em, smash 'em, smash 'em.
Then you spread 'em, you spread 'em. *(pretend to spread berries)*
Spread 'em, spread 'em, spread 'em.

Chorus

Then you take the sandwich and
You bite it, you bite it. *(pretend to bite a sandwich)*
Bite it, bite it, bite it.
Then you chew it, you chew it. *(pretend to chew a sandwich)*
Chew it, chew it, chew it.
Then you swallow it, you swallow it. *(pretend to swallow peanut butter sandwich)*
Swallow it, swallow it, swallow it.

Hum chorus.

Theme Connections

Cooking
Food

Peanut Sitting on a Railroad Track

(Tune: Polly Wolly Doodle)

A peanut sat on a railroad track,
His heart was all a-flutter.
Then round the bend came a railroad train.
Toot! Toot! Peanut butter!
Squish!

Theme Connections

Food
Humor
Trains

Peas Porridge Hot

(make up a partner clap)
Peas porridge hot
Peas porridge cold,
Peas porridge in the pot
Nine days old.
Some like it hot.
Some like it cold.
Some like in the pot
Nine days old!

Theme Connections

Food
Opposites

Peter Piper

Peter Piper picked a peck of pickled peppers;
A peck of pickled peppers Peter Piper picked;
If Peter Piper picked a peck of pickled peppers,
Where's the peck of pickled peppers Peter Piper picked?

Theme Connections

Food
Sounds of Language

The Pettitoes

The pettitoes are little feet, *(tap feet together)*
And the little feet are not big.
Great feet belong to the grunting hog, *(snort like a hog)*
And the pettitoes to the little pig. *(say "wee, wee, wee")*

Theme Connections

Opposites
Pigs

A Pie Sat on a Pear Tree

A pie sat on a pear tree,
A pie sat on a pear tree,
A pie sat on a pear tree,
Heigh ho, heigh ho, heigh ho.
And once so merrily hopped she,
And twice so merrily hopped she,
And thrice so merrily hopped she.
Heigh ho, heigh ho, heigh ho.

Theme Connections

Counting
Food
Numbers

Pinkety, Pinkety

Pinkety, pinkety thumb to thumb *(put thumbs on each other)*
Wish a wish and it's sure to come. *(make a silent wish)*
If yours comes true, mine will come true.
Pinkety pinkety thumb to thumb. *(put thumbs on each other)*

Theme Connections

Parts of the Body

Pipe, Cat

Pipe, cat,
Dance, mouse
We'll have a wedding at our good house.

Theme Connections

Cats
Celebrations
Houses and Homes
Mice
Music

Point to the Right

Point to the right of me.
Point to the left of me.
Point up above me.
Point down below.
Right, left, up,
And down so slow.

Use both arms and follow the actions slowly. Slowly speed up at the end.

Theme Connections

Movement
Opposites
Spatial Relationships

Polly Put the Kettle On

Polly, put the kettle on,
Polly, put the kettle on,
Polly, put the kettle on,
We'll all have tea.

Sukey, take it off again,
Sukey, take it off again,
Sukey, take it off again,
They've all gone away.

Theme Connections

Cooking
Food

Blow the fire and make the toast,
Put the muffins on to roast.
Who is going to eat the most?
We'll all have tea.

Polly Wolly Doodle

Oh, I went down south
For to see my Sal
Sing Polly wolly doodle all the day.
My Sal, she is
A spunky gal,
Sing Polly wolly doodle all the day.

Chorus:
Fare thee well,
Fare thee well,
Fare thee well my fairy fay
For I'm going to Lou'siana
For to see my Susyanna
Sing Polly wolly doodle all the day

Oh, my Sal, she is
A maiden fair,
Sing Polly wolly doodle all the day,
With curly eyes
And laughing hair,
Sing Polly wolly doodle all the day.

Chorus

Behind the barn,
Down on my knees
Sing Polly wolly doodle all the day.
I thought I heard
A chicken sneeze,
Sing Polly wolly doodle all the day.

Chorus

He sneezed so hard
With the whooping cough,
Sing Polly wolly doodle all the day.

He sneezed his head
And his tail right off,
Sing Polly wolly doodle all the day.

Chorus

Oh, a grasshopper sittin'
On a railroad track,
Sing Polly wolly doodle all the day,
A-pickin' his teeth
With a carpet tack,
Sing Polly wolly doodle all the day.

Chorus

Oh, I went to bed
But it wasn't any use,
Sing Polly wolly doodle all the day.
My feet stuck out
Like a chicken roost,
Sing Polly wolly doodle all the day.

Chorus

Theme Connections

Friends
Humor

Pop! Goes the Weasel

All around the cobbler's bench
The monkey chased the weasel.
The monkey thought 'twas all in fun—
Pop! Goes the weasel.

Johnny has the whooping cough,
Mary has the measles.
That's the way the money goes—
Pop! Goes the weasel.

A penny for a spool of thread
A penny for a needle.
That's the way the money goes—
Pop! Goes the weasel.

All around the mulberry bush,
The monkey chased the weasel.
That's the way the money goes—
Pop! Goes the weasel.

Theme Connections

Humor
Money
Monkeys
Weasels

Porridge Is Bubbling

Porridge is bubbling, bubbling hot.
Stir it round and round in the pot,
The bubbles plip.
The bubbles plop.
It's ready to eat all bubbling hot.
Wake up, baby.
Wake up soon.
We'll eat the porridge with a spoon.

Theme Connections

Babies
Cooking
Food
Sounds of Language

Pretty Butterfly

Yesterday I went to the field.
I saw a beautiful butterfly. *(pretend to study a butterfly)*
But on seeing me so close,
It flew away ever so quickly. *(make fluttering movements)*

Theme Connections

Butterflies

Pretty Maid, Pretty Maid

Pretty maid, pretty maid,
Where have you been?
Gathering a pony to give to the Queen.
Pretty maid, pretty maid,
What gave she you?
She gave me a diamond as big as my shoe.

Theme Connections

Kings and Queens
Ponies

Puddin' 'n' Tame

What's your name?
Puddin 'n' tame.
Ask me again,
And I'll tell you the same.

What's your name?
Puddin 'n' tame.
Where do you live?
In a sieve.

Theme Connection

Humor

Punchinello

What can you do,
Punchinello, funny fellow?
What can you do,
Punchinello, funny you?

We can do it, too,
Punchinello, funny fellow,
We can do it, too,
Punchinello, funny you!

You choose one of us,
Punchinello, funny fellow,
You choose one of us,
Punchinello, funny you!

*Children form into a circle, with one child in center as
    "Punchinello."*
*Verse 1: Punchinello does an action, such as hopping on
    one foot or twirling in place while the children in the
    circle sing.*
*Verse 2: The children in the circle copy the action that
    Punchinello is doing.*
*Verse 3: Punchinello selects a child to be the next
    Punchinello, then takes that child's place in the circle.*

Theme Connections

Movement
Self-esteem

Puppet Clown

Puppet clown, puppet clown,
Moving up and down and round.
Puppet clown, puppet clown,
You do make such silly sounds!
Puppet clown, puppet clown,
How you shake and dance and wiggle!
Puppet clown, puppet clown,
How you make me laugh and giggle!

Theme Connections

Emotions
Movement
Spatial Relationships

Puppies and Kittens

One little, two little, three little kittens *(pop up three fingers)*
Were napping in the sun. *(rest head on hands)*
One little, two little, three little puppies *(pop up three fingers)*
Said, "Let's have some fun." *(smile)*

Up to the kittens the puppies went creeping *(creep right
    fingers up left arm)*
As quiet as could be.
One little, two little, three little kittens
Went scampering up a tree! *(wiggle fingers overhead)*

Theme Connections

Cats   Movement
Counting   Numbers
Dogs

Pussy at the Fireside

Pussy at the fireside suppin up brose,
Down came a cinder and burned pussy's nose.
Oh, said Pussy, that's no fair!
Well, said the cinder, you shouldn't be there.

Theme Connection

Cats

Pussy Cat

Pussy cat sits beside the fire
So pretty and so fair.
In walks the little dog,
Ah, Pussy, are you there?
How do you do, Mistress Pussy,
Mistress Pussy, how do you do?
I thank you kindly little dog,
I'm very well just now.

Theme Connections

Cats
Dogs

Pussy Cat Ate the Dumplings

Pussy cat ate the dumplings,
Pussy cat ate the dumplings.
Mama stood by, and cried, "Oh, fie!
Why did you eat the dumplings?"

Theme Connections

Cats
Emotions
Food

Pussy Cat Mew

Pussy cat mew jumped over a coal,
And in her best petticoat burnt a great hole.
Pussy cat mew shall have no more milk,
'Til her best petticoat's mended with silk.

Theme Connections

Cats
Clothing

Pussycat, Pussycat

Pussycat, pussycat,
Where have you been?
I've been to London
To look at the Queen.

Pussycat, pussycat,
What did you there?
I frightened a little mouse
Under the chair.

Theme Connections

Cats
Kings and Queens
Mice

Queen of Hearts

The Queen of Hearts,
She made some tarts,
All on a summer's day;
The Knave of Hearts,
He stole those tarts,
And took them clean away.

The King of Hearts
Called for the tarts,
And beat the Knave full sore;
The Knave of Hearts
Brought back the tarts,
And vowed he'd steal no more.

Theme Connections

Food
Kings and Queens
Shapes

Rain
by Robert Louis Stevenson

The rain is raining all around,
It falls on field and tree,
It rains on the umbrellas here,
And on the ships at sea.

Theme Connection

Weather

Rain
(on the green grass)

Rain on the green grass
And rain on the tree;
Rain on the housetop
But not on me.

Theme Connection

Weather

The Rain
(splish, splash)

Splish, splash,
Splish, splash,
Drip, drop,
Drip, drop,
Will the rain ever stop?

Theme Connections

Rain
Sounds of Language
Weather

Rain, Rain, Go Away

Rain, rain, go away,
Come again another day.
Little (child's name) wants to play.
Rain, rain, go away.

Variation

Rain, rain, go away,
This is mother's washing day
Rain, rain, pour down
Wash my mother's nightgown.

Theme Connection

Weather

Raindrop Song

If all the raindrops *(wiggle fingers in the air)*
Were lemon drops and gum drops   *(tap one index finger
   against palm of other hand)*
Oh, what a rain that would be! *(wiggle fingers in the air)*
Standing outside, with my mouth open wide.
Ah-ah-ah-ah-ah-ah-ah-ah-ah-ah! *(stand, looking up with
   mouth open)*
If all the raindrops
Were lemon drops and gum drops,
Oh, what a rain that would be!

If all the snowflakes
Were candy bars and milkshakes,
Oh, what a snow that would be!
Standing outside with my mouth open wide.
Ah-ah-ah-ah-ah-ah-ah-ah-ah-ah!
If all the snowflakes
Were candy bars and milkshakes,
Oh, what a snow that would be!

If all the sunbeams
Were bubble gum and ice cream,
Oh, what a sun that would be!
Standing outside with my mouth open wide.
Ah-ah-ah-ah-ah-ah-ah-ah-ah-ah!
If all the sunbeams
Were bubble gum and ice cream
Oh, what a sun that would be!

Theme Connections

Food
Humor
Weather

Rat-a-Tat-Tat

Rat-a-tat-tat, who is that?
Only grandma's pussy cat.
What do you want?
A pint of milk.
Where's your money?
In my pocket.
Where's your pocket?
I forgot it.
Oh, you silly pussy cat.

Theme Connections

Cats
Money
Sounds of Language

Red Dress

Sally's wearing a red dress, red dress, red dress,
Sally's wearing a red dress all day long.

Theme Connections

Clothes
Colors

Red River Valley

From this valley they say you are going,
We will miss your bright eyes and sweet smile,
For they say you are taking the sunshine
Which has brightened our pathway a while.

Come and sit by my side if you love me,
Do not hasten to bid me adieu.
But remember the Red River Valley
And the one who has loved you so true.

Won't you think of the valley you're leaving?
O how lonely, how sad it will be.
O think of the fond heart you're breaking,
And the grief you are causing to me.

As you go to your home by the ocean,
May you never forget those sweet hours
That we spent in the Red River Valley,
And the love we exchange 'mid the flowers.

Theme Connections

Emotions
Oceans and Seas

Red, White, and Blue

Red, white, and blue,
Tap me on the shoe. *(tap shoe or foot)*
Red, white, and green,
Tap me on the bean. *(tap head)*
Red, white, and black,
Tap me on the back. *(tap back)*
All out!

Theme Connections

Colors
Movement
Parts of the Body

Ride a Cockhorse to Banbury Cross

Ride a cockhorse to Banbury Cross,
To see a fine lady upon a white horse;
Rings on her fingers and bells on her toes,
And so she makes music wherever she goes.

Variation

Ride a cock horse to Banbury Cross
To see what Tommy can buy.
A penny white loaf, a penny white cake
And a two-penny apple pie.

Ride a cock horse to Banbury Cross
To buy little Johnny a galloping horse.
It trots behind, and it ambles before,
And Johnny shall ride till he can ride no more.

Theme Connections

Horses
Music

A Rig-a-Jig-Jig

As I was walking down the street, down the street,
  down the street,
A very good friend I chanced to meet,
Hi-ho, hi-ho, hi-ho!

A rig-a-jig-jig and away we go, away we go, away we go!
A rig-a-jig-jig and away we go,
Hi-ho, hi-ho, hi-ho!

*Choose one child to walk first, that child chooses a friend to
rig-a-jig-jig with; then the first child sits down and the second child walks.*

Theme Connections

Friends
Movement

Rindle, Randle

Rindle, randle, light the candle,
The cat's among the pies.
No matter for that, the cat'll get fat,
And I'm too lazy to rise.

Theme Connections

Cats
Food

Ring Around the Rosie

Ring around the rosie
A pocket full of posies
Ashes, ashes, we all fall down!

The children circle around, singing the chant. At the end of the verse, they do what the song says, and all fall down.

Variation

Ring-a-ring o' roses,
A pocket full of posies,
A-tishoo, A-tishoo,
We all fall down.

Ring -ring-roses,
A pocket full of posies,
One for you and one for me,
And one for little Moses.

A-tishoo, a-tishoo,
We'll all fall down.
Ring-ring-a roses,
A pocket full of poses.

Theme Connections

Flowers
Movement

River

Runs all day and never walks,
Often murmurs, never talks,
It has a bed but never sleeps,
It has a mouth but never eats.
(a river)

Theme Connections

Humor
Nature
Rivers

Robert Rowley Rolled a Round

Robert Rowley rolled a round roll 'round;
A round roll Robert Rowley rolled 'round.
If Robert Rowley rolled a round roll 'round,
Where rolled the round roll Robert Rowley rolled 'round?

Theme Connections

Humor
Shapes
Sounds of Language

Robin and Richard

Robin and Richard were two pretty men.
They lay in bed till the clock struck ten.
Then up starts Robin and looks at the sky.
Oh, brother Richard, the sun's very high.
The steamer has gone, we can't get a ride
You carry the wallet, I'll run by your side.

Theme Connections

Families
Time of Day

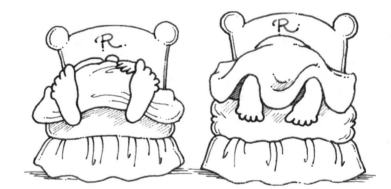

Rockabye, Baby

Rockabye, baby, in the tree top,
When the wind blows, the cradle
   will rock.
When the bough breaks, the cradle
   will fall,
And down will come baby, cradle
   and all.

Variation

Hush-a-bye, baby, in the tree top,
When the wind blows, the cradle will rock.
When the bough breaks, the cradle will fall,
And down will come baby, cradle and all.

Hush-a-bye, baby, way up on high,
Never mind, baby, mommy is nigh,
Swinging the baby all around.
Hush-a-bye, baby, up hill and down.

Theme Connections

Babies
Families

Rock-a-Bye, Thy Cradle Is Green

Rock-a-bye baby, thy cradle is green;
Father's a nobleman, mother's a queen.
And Betty's a lady and wears a gold ring,
And Johnny's a drummer and drums for the king.

Theme Connections

Babies
Kings and Queens

Rock-a-My-Soul

Oh, a rock-a-my-soul in the bosom of Abraham,
Rock-a-my soul in the bosom of Abraham,
Rock-a-my soul in the bosom of Abraham,
Oh, rock-a-my soul.

So high, you can't get over it,
So low, you can't get under it,
So wide, you can't get around it,
Oh, rock-a-my soul.

Theme Connections

Opposites
Spatial Relationships

The Rose Is Red,
The Violet's Blue

The rose is red, the violet's blue,
The honey's sweet, and so are you.
Thou art my love and I am thine;
I drew thee to be my Valentine.
The lot was cast and then I drew,
And fortune said it should be you.

Theme Connections

Celebrations
Colors
Emotions
Holidays

Roses Are Red

Roses are red,
Violets are blue.
Sugar is sweet
And so are you.

Roses are red,
Violets are blue.
Grass is green,
And so are you.

Theme Connections

Celebrations
Colors
Holidays
Humor

Round and Round

Round and round the butter dish,
One, two, three.
If you want a pretty girl,
Just pick me.

Theme Connections

Counting
Numbers
Self-esteem
Shapes

Round and Round the Garden

Round and round the garden like a teddy bear. *(swirl index finger in palm of other hand)*
One step, two steps, *(walk fingers up arm)*
Hidden under there! *(walk fingers under arm)*

Theme Connections

Movement
Shapes
Teddy Bears

Round the Maypole

Round and round the maypole
Merrily we go.
Singing hip-a-cherry
Dancing as we go.
All the happy children
Upon the village green,
Sitting in the sunshine
Hurrah for the queen.

Theme Connections

Celebrations
Kings and Queens
Movement
Weather

Row, Row, Row Your Boat

Row, row, row your boat
Gently down the stream.
Merrily, merrily, merrily, merrily,
Life is but a dream.

Theme Connections

Boats and Ships
Emotions
Rivers

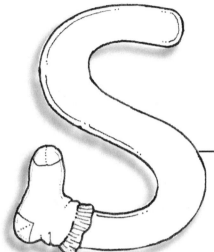

Sailing, Sailing

Sailing, sailing over the bounding main,
Many a stormy wind shall blow
'Ere Jack comes home again.

Sailing, sailing over the bounding main,
For many a stormy wind shall blow
'Ere Jack comes home again.

Theme Connections

Boats and Ships
Weather

A Sailor Went to Sea

A sailor went to sea, sea, sea.
To see what she could see, see, see.
But all that she could see, see, see.
Was the bottom of the deep blue sea, sea, sea.

Theme Connections

Boats and Ships
Oceans and Seas
Sounds of Language

Sally Go Round the Sun

Sally, go 'round the sun.
Sally, go 'round the moon.
Sally, go 'round the chimney pots
On a Sunday afternoon.

Theme Connections

Days of the Week
Sun, Moon, Stars
Time of Day

Sam, Sam

Sam, Sam, the butcher man,
Washed his face in a frying pan.
Combed his hair with a wagon wheel,
And died with a toothache in his heel.

Variation

The Waffle Man is a fine old man.
He washes his face in a frying pan.
He makes his waffles with his hand.
Everybody loves the Waffle Man.

Theme Connections

Humor   Occupations

Say and Touch

Say "red," and touch your head.
Say "sky," and touch your eye.
Say "bear," and touch your hair.
Say "hear," and touch your ear.
Say "south," and touch your mouth.
Say "rose," and touch your nose.
Say "in," and touch your chin.
Say "rest," and touch your chest.
Say "farm," and touch your arm.
Say "yummy," and touch your tummy.
Say "bee," and touch your knee.
Say "neat," and touch your feet.

Theme Connections

Parts of the Body   Sounds of Language

Say, Say, My Playmate

Say, say, my playmate,
Come out and play with me,
And bring your dollies three.
Climb up my apple tree.
Look down my rain barrel.
Slide down my cellar door,
And we'll be jolly friends
Forever more, 1-2-3-4.

It was a rainy day,
She couldn't come out and play.
With tearful eyes, she breathed a sigh
And I could hear her say:
Say, say, my playmate,
I cannot play with you.
My dolly's got the flu
Boo hoo hoo hoo hoo hoo.

Ain't got no rainbow
Ain't got no cellar door
But we'll be jolly friends
Forever more, 1-2-3-4.

Theme Connections

Emotions
Friends

Scarborough Fair

Are you going to Scarborough Fair?
Parsley, sage, rosemary, and thyme.
Remember me to one who lives there,
She once was a true love of mine.

Tell her to make me a cambric shirt,
Parsley, sage, rosemary and thyme.
Without a seam or fine needlework,
Then, she'll be a true love of mine.

Theme Connection

Emotions

Seasons

In the summer leaves are rustling,
Green, green leaves are rustling.
In the summer leaves are rustling,
Rustling in the trees.

In the autumn leaves are falling,
Brown, brown, leaves are falling.
In the summer leaves are falling,
Falling from the trees.

Theme Connections

Colors
Nature
Seasons

In the winter leaves are sleeping,
Brown, brown leaves are sleeping.
In the winter leaves are sleeping,
Sleeping in the trees.

The Secret

We have a secret, just we three,
The robin, and I, and the sweet cherry-tree;
The bird told the tree, and the tree told me,
And nobody knows it but just us three.

But of course the robin knows it best,
Because he built the—I shan't tell the rest;
And laid the four little—something in it—
I'm afraid I shall tell it every minute.

But if the tree and the robin don't peep,
I'll try my best the secret to keep;
Though I know when the little birds fly about
Then the whole secret will be out.

We have a secret, just we three,
The robin, and I, and the sweet cherry-tree;
The bird told the tree, and the tree told me,
And nobody knows it but just us three.

Theme Connections

Birds
Humor
Nature

See a Pin

See a pin and pick it up,
All day long you'll have good luck.
See a pin and let it lay,
Bad luck you'll have all the day.

Theme Connection

Opposites

See-Saw, Margery Daw

See-saw, Margery Daw,
Jenny shall have a new master;
And she shall have but a penny a day,
Because she can't work any faster.

Theme Connections

Money
Work

See-Saw, Millie McGraw

See-saw, Millie McGraw,
Rocking slow,
Back and forth we go.
See-saw, Millie McGraw.

Theme Connection

Opposites

See Saw, Sacradown

See Saw, sacradown
Which is the way to London town?
One foot up and the other foot down
That is the way to London town.
And just the same, over dale and hill
Is also the way to wherever you will.

Theme Connection

Opposites

September Blow Soft

September blow soft
Till the fruit's in the loft.

Theme Connection

Seasons

She Is Handsome

She is handsome, she is pretty.
She is the girl of the golden city.
She goes a-courting, one, two, three.
Please and tell me who is she?

Theme Connection

Counting

She Sells Seashells

She sells seashells by the seashore
By the seashore she sells seashells.

Theme Connections

Oceans and Seas
Sounds of Language

She Waded in the Water

(Tune: Battle Hymn of the Republic)

She waded in the water and she got her feet all wet,
She waded in the water and she got her feet all wet,
She waded in the water and she got her feet all wet,
But she didn't get her (clap, clap) wet (clap) yet. (clap)

Chorus:
Glory, glory, hallelujah!
Glory, glory, hallelujah!
Glory, glory, hallelujah!
But she didn't get her (clap, clap) wet (clap) yet. (clap)

Theme Connections

Parts of the Body
Seasons

She waded in the water and she got her ankles wet (3 times)
But she didn't get her (clap, clap) wet, (clap) yet. (clap)

Chorus

She waded in the water and she got her knees all wet…
She waded in the water and she got her thighs all wet…
She waded in the water and she finally got it wet…
She finally got her bathing suit wet!

She'll Be Comin' 'Round the Mountain

She'll be comin' 'round the mountain when she comes.
She'll be comin' 'round the mountain when she comes.—
"Toot, toot"
She'll be comin' 'round the mountain,
She'll be comin' 'round the mountain,
She'll be comin' 'round the mountain when she comes.—
"Toot, toot" *(pull an imaginary whistle)*

She'll be driving six white horses when she comes.—"Whoa
  back!" *(pull back reins)*
She'll be driving six white horses when she comes.
She'll be driving six white horses,
She'll be driving six white horses,
She'll be driving six white horses when she comes.—"Whoa
  back!" *(pull back reins)*

And we'll all go out to meet her when she comes.—"Hi,
  babe!" *(wave hand in greeting)*
And we'll all go out to meet her when she comes.
And we'll all go out to meet her,
And we'll all go out to meet her,
And we'll all go out to meet her when she comes.—"Hi,
  babe!" *(wave hand in greeting)*

We will all have chicken and dumplin's when she comes.—
  "Yum, yum" *(rub tummy)*
We will all have chicken and dumplin's when she comes.
We will all have chicken and dumplin's,
We will all have chicken and dumplin's,
We will all have chicken and dumplin's when she comes.—
  "Yum, yum" *(rub tummy)*

She'll be wearing red pajamas when she comes.—
"Scratch, scratch." *(scratch)*
She'll be wearing red pajamas when she comes.—
"Scratch, scratch." *(scratch)*
She'll be wearing red pajamas,
She'll be wearing red pajamas,
She'll be wearing red pajamas when she
comes. —"Scratch, scratch" *(scratch)*

She'll have to sleep with Grandma when she
comes.—"Move over" *(make pushing motions)*
She'll have to sleep with Grandma when she comes.
She'll have to sleep with Grandma,
She'll have to sleep with Grandma,
She'll have to sleep with Grandma when she
comes.— "Move over" *(make pushing motion)*

We'll have a great big party when she comes.—
"Yahoo!" *(swing arm over head for a lasso)*
We'll have a great big party when she comes.
We'll have a great big party,
We'll have a great big party,
We'll have a great big party when she comes.—"Yahoo!"
   (swing arm over head for a lasso)

On the last line of each verse, perform the actions for that
verse and all preceding ones. For example, at the end of the
last verse say and do the actions for "Yahoo; move over;
scratch, scratch; yum, yum; hi, babe; whoa back; and toot,
toot."

Theme Connections

Celebrations   Horses
Families   Humor
Food

Shoo Fly

Shoo fly, don't bother me
Shoo fly, don't bother me
Shoo fly, don't bother me
I belong to somebody.

Variation

Shoo, fly, don't bother me
Shoo, fly, don't bother me
Shoo, fly, don't bother me
For I belong to somebody.

I feel, I feel,
I feel like a morning star,
I feel, I feel,
I feel like a morning star.

Theme Connections

Flies

Short'nin' Bread

Put on the skillet,
Slip on the lid,
Mama's gonna make
A little short'nin' bread.
That ain't all
She's gonna do,
Mama's gonna make
A little coffee, too.

Refrain:
Mama's little baby loves
Short'nin', short'nin',
Mama's little baby loves
Short'nin' bread,
Mama's little baby loves
Short'nin', short'nin',
Mama's little baby loves
Short'nin' bread.

Three little children
Lyin' in bed.
Two were sick
And the other 'most dead.
Sent for the doctor
And the doctor said,
"Give those children some
Short'nin' bread."

Refrain

When those children,
Sick in bed,
Heard that talk
About short'nin' bread,
Popped up well

To dance and sing,
Skipped around and cut
The pigeon wing.

Refrain

Theme Connections

Cooking
Families
Food
Occupations

Simple Gifts

'Tis a gift to be simple, 'tis a gift to be free,
'Tis a gift to come down to where we ought to be,
And when we find ourselves in the place just right,
'Twill be in the valley of love and delight.

When true simplicity is gained,
To bow and to bend we won't be ashamed.
To turn, to turn, will be our delight
'Til by turning and turning we come around right.

Theme Connection

Emotions

Simple Simon

Simple Simon met a pieman
Going to the fair;
Says Simple Simon to the pieman,
"Let me taste your ware."

Says the pieman to Simple Simon,
"Show me first your penny,"
Says Simple Simon to the pieman,
"Indeed, I have not any."

Simple Simon went a-fishing,
For to catch a whale.
All the water he had got
Was in his mother's pail.

Variation

Simple Simon met a pieman,
Going to the fair.
Said Simple Simon to the pieman,
"Let me taste your ware."

Said the pieman unto Simon,
"Show me first your penny."
Said Simple Simon to the pieman,
"Indeed I have not any."

Simple Simon went a-fishing
For to catch a whale.
All the water he had got
Was in his mother's pail.

Simple Simon went to look
If plums grew on a thistle;
He pricked his fingers very much,
Which made poor Simon whistle.

He went for water in a sieve,
But soon it all fell through;
And now poor Simon
Bids you all adieu.

Theme Connections

Food
Money

Sing a Song of Sixpence

Sing a song of sixpence,
A pocket full of rye;
Four-and-twenty blackbirds
Baked in a pie!

When the pie was opened
The birds began to sing:
Was not that a dainty dish
To set before the king?

The king was in his counting-house,
Counting out his money;
The queen was in the parlor,
Eating bread and honey.

The maid was in the garden,
Hanging out the clothes;
When down came a blackbird,
And snapped off her nose.

As it fell upon the ground
'Twas spied by Jenny Wren,
Who took a stick of sealing wax
And stuck it on again.

As they saw the nose stuck on
The maids cried out "Hooray!"
Till someone said, "But it is stuck
The topsy-turvy way!"

They took her to the King,
Who just replied, "What stuff!"
'Tis better far put on that way,
So nice for taking snuff!"

They bought a pound of Lundy foot*
And threw it in her face.
She sneezed, "Achoo!" which twisted it
Into its proper place.

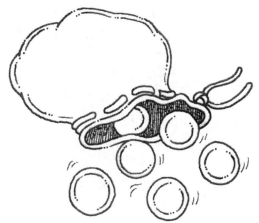

Theme Connections

Birds
Humor
Kings and Queens
Money

*Lundy foot is a variety of snuff.

Sing, Sing

Sing, sing, what shall I sing?
The cat's run away with the pudding string.
Do, do, what shall I do?
The cat's run away with the pudding too.

Theme Connections

Cats
Food

Sippin' Cider Through a Straw

The prettiest girl
(The prettiest girl)
I ever saw
(I ever saw)
Was sippin' ci-
(Was sippin' ci-)
Der through a straw
(Der through a straw)

The prettiest girl I ever saw
Was sippin' cider through a straw.

I told that gal
(I told that gal)
I didn't see how
(I didn't see how)
She sipped that ci-
(She sipped that ci-)
Der through a straw
(Der through a straw)

I told that gal I didn't see how
She sipped that cider through a straw.

Then cheek to cheek
(Then cheek to cheek)
And jaw to jaw
(And jaw to jaw)
We sipped that ci-
(We sipped that ci-)
Der through a straw
(Der through a straw)

Then cheek to cheek and jaw to jaw
We sipped that cider through a straw.

And now and then
(And now and then)
That straw would slip
(That straw would slip)
And I'd sip some ci-
(And I'd sip some ci-)
Der from her lip
(Der from her lip)

And now and then that straw would slip
And I'd sip some cider from her lip.

And now I've got
(And now I've got)
A mother-in-law
(A mother-in-law)
From sippin' ci-
(From sippin' ci-)
Der through a straw
(Der through a straw)

And now I've got a mother-in-law
From sippin' cider through a straw.

The moral of
(The moral of)
This little tale
(This little tale)
Is to sip your soda
(Is to sip your soda)
Through a pail
(Through a pail)

The moral of this little tale is to sip your soda
through a pail!

Theme Connections

Friends
Humor

Sippity Sup, Sippity Sup

Sippity sup, sippity sup,
Bread and milk from a china cup.
Bread and milk from a bright silver spoon
Made of a piece of the bright silver moon.
Sippity sup, sippity sup,
Sippity, sippity sup.

Theme Connections

Food
Sun, Moon, Stars

Six Little Snowmen

Six little snowmen all made of snow. *(hold up six fingers)*
Six little snowmen standing in a row.

Out came the sun and stayed all day. *(lift arms over head in a circle)*
One little snowman melted away. *(pretend to melt to the floor)*
Five little snowmen all made of snow.

Continue until all of the snowmen have melted.

Theme Connections

Counting
Numbers
Seasons
Sun, Moon, Stars
Weather

Six White Ducks

Six white ducks that I once knew,
Fat ducks, skinny ducks, they were, too.
But the one little duck with the feather on her back,
She ruled the others with a quack, quack, quack!

Down to the river they would go,
Wibble, wobble, wibble, wobble all in a row.
But the one little duck with the feather on her back,
She ruled the others with a quack, quack, quack!

Theme Connections

Animal Sounds
Counting
Ducks
Numbers
Rivers

Skidamarink

Skidamarink a dink a dink,
Skidamarink a doo,
I love you.
Skidamarink a dink a dink,
Skidamarink a doo,
I love you.

I love you in the morning
And in the afternoon,
I love you in the evening
And underneath the moon;
Oh, Skidamarink a dink a dink,
Skidamarink a doo
I love you!

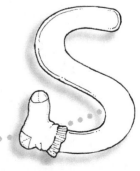

Variation

Skinnamarinky dinky dink, *(hold right elbow in left hand, wave fingers)*
Skinnamarinky doo, *(hold left elbow in right hand, wave fingers)*
I love you. *(point to eye, heart, and to other person)*
Skinnamarinky dinky dink,
Skinnamarinky doo,
I love you.

Theme Connections

Emotions
Time of Day
Sun, Moon, Stars

Skip to My Lou

Skip, skip, skip to my Lou,
Skip, skip, skip to my Lou,
Skip, skip, skip to my Lou,
Skip to my Lou, my darlin'.

Fly's in the buttermilk,
Shoo, fly, shoo,
Fly's in the buttermilk,

Shoo, fly, shoo,
Fly's in the buttermilk,
Shoo, fly, shoo,
Skip to my Lou, my darlin'.

Refrain:
Skip, skip, skip to my Lou,
Skip, skip, skip to my Lou,
Skip, skip, skip to my Lou,
Skip to my Lou, my darlin'.

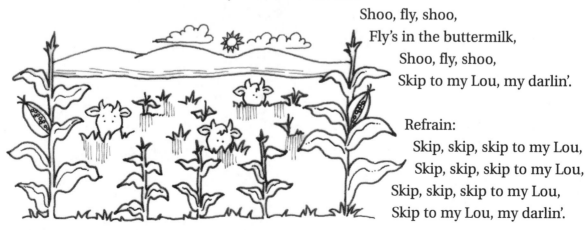

Cows in the cornfield,
What'll I do?
Cows in the cornfield,
What'll I do?
Cows in the cornfield,
What'll I do?
Skip to my Lou, my darlin'.

Refrain

There's a little red wagon,
Paint it blue.
There's a little red wagon,
Paint it blue.
There's a little red wagon,
Paint it blue.
Skip to my Lou, my darlin'.

Refrain

Variation

Lost my partner, what'll I do?
Lost my partner, what'll I do?
Lost my partner, what'll I do?
Skip to my lou, my darlin'.

Refrain:
Skip, skip, skip to my Lou,
Skip, skip, skip to my Lou,
Skip, skip, skip to my Lou,
Skip to my Lou, my darlin'.

I'll get another one, prettier than you,
I'll get another one, prettier than you,
I'll get another one, prettier than you,
Skip to my Lou, my darlin'.

Refrain

Can't get a red bird, jay bird'll do,
Can't get a red bird, jay bird'll do,
Can't get a red bird, jay bird'll do,
Skip to my Lou, my darlin'.

Refrain

Fly's in the buttermilk, shoo, fly, shoo,
Fly's in the buttermilk, shoo, fly, shoo,
Fly's in the buttermilk, shoo, fly, shoo,
Skip to my Lou, my darlin'.

Refrain

Cat's in the cream jar, ooh, ooh, ooh,
Cat's in the cream jar, ooh, ooh, ooh
Cat's in the cream jar, ooh, ooh, ooh,
Skip to my Lou, my darlin'.

Refrain

Off to Texas, two by two,
Off to Texas, two by two,
Off to Texas, two by two,
Skip to my Lou, my darlin'.

Refrain

Theme Connections

Colors
Cows
Flies
Movement

Sleep, Baby, Sleep

Sleep, baby, sleep,
Your father tends the sheep.
Your mother shakes the dreamland tree.
Down falls a dream for thee.
Sleep, baby, sleep.

Variation

Sleep, baby, sleep,
Thy papa guards the sheep.
Thy mama shakes the dreamland tree
And from it falls sweet dreams for thee.

Sleep, baby, sleep,
Sleep, baby, sleep,
Our cottage vale is deep;
The little lamb is on the green,
With woolly fleece so soft and clean.

Sleep, baby, sleep,
Sleep, baby, sleep,
Down where the woodbines creep;
Be always like the lamb so mild,
A kind and sweet and gentle child.

Theme Connections

Babies
Lullabies
Naptime/Sleeping

Slip on Your Raincoat

Slip on your raincoat,
Pull on your galoshes;
Wading in puddles
Makes splishes and sploshes.

Theme Connection

Weather

Slippery Soap

Slippery, slippery, slippery soap
Now you see it and now you don't.
Slide it on the arms,
One, two, three.
Now your arms are slippery.
Slide it on the legs,
One, two, three.
Now your legs are slippery.

Repeat the verse substituting different body parts.

Theme Connections

Counting
Numbers
Parts of the Body
Self-esteem

Slowly, Slowly

Slowly, slowly, very slowly *(walk fingers up arm slowly)*
Creeps the garden snail.
Slowly, slowly, very slowly
Up the wooden rail.

Quickly, quickly, very quickly *(run fingers up arm)*
Runs the little mouse.
Quickly, quickly, very quickly
Round about the house.

Theme Connections

Fast and Slow
Mice
Opposites
Snails

Smiling Girls

Smiling girls, rosy boys
Come and buy my little toys.
Monkeys made of gingerbread,
And sugar horses painted red.

Theme Connections

Colors
Toys

A Snail

A snail crept up the lily's stalk:
"How nice and smooth," said he;
"It's quite a pleasant evening walk,
And just the thing for me!"

Theme Connections

    Flowers
    Snails
    Time of Day

Snail, Snail

Snail, snail, put out your horns, *(make a fist, thumb tucked inside; lift little finger and index finger to make horns)*
And I'll give you bread and barley corns.

Theme Connections

    Food
    Snails

Snow, Snow, Fly Away

Snow, snow, fly away
Over the hills and far away.

Theme Connection

Weather

Snowman

I made a little snowman,
I made him big and round.
I made him from a snowball,
I rolled upon the ground.
He has two eyes, a nose, a mouth,
A lovely scarf of red.
He even has some buttons,
And a hat upon his head.
Melt, melt, melt, melt
Melt, melt, melt, melt

Theme Connections

Parts of the Body
Seasons
Weather

Snowman
(as round as a ball)

This is a snowman as round as a ball.
He has two large eyes, but he's not very tall.
If the sun shines down on him today,
My jolly snowman will melt away.

Theme Connections

Seasons
Sun, Moon, Stars
Weather

Soda Bread

Soda bread and soft bread,
Crazy bread and hard bread,
Loaf bread, cornbread,
Plain bread and biscuits.

Theme Connections

Food
Opposites

Solomon Grundy

Solomon Grundy,
Born on Monday,
Christened on Tuesday,
Married on Wednesday,
Took ill on Thursday,
Worse on Friday,
Died on Saturday,
Buried on Sunday:
This is the end
Of Solomon Grundy.

Theme Connection

Days of the Week

Sometimes

Sometimes I am tall, *(stand tall)*
Sometimes I am small. *(crouch low)*
Sometimes I am very, very, tall. *(stand on tiptoes)*
Sometimes I am very, very small. *(crouch and lower head)*
Sometimes tall, *(stand tall)*
Sometimes small. *(crouch down)*
Sometimes neither tall nor small. *(stand normally)*

Theme Connections

Movement
Opposites
Self-esteem

Spring Is Coming

Spring is coming, spring is coming!
How do you think I know?
I see a flower blooming,
I know it must be so.
Spring is coming, spring is coming!
How do you think I know?
I see a blossom on the tree,
I know it must be so.

Theme Connections

Flowers
Nature
Seasons

Spring Is Showery

Spring is showery, flowery, bowery.
Summer hoppy, croppy, poppy.
Autumn slippy, drippy, nippy.
Winter breezy, sneezy, freezy.

Theme Connections

Seasons
Sounds of Language

The Squirrel

Whisky, frisky,
Hippity hop,
Up he goes
To the tree top!

Whirly, twirly,
Round and round,
Down he scampers
To the ground.

Furly, curly,
What a tail!
Tall as a feather,
Broad as a sail!

Where's his supper?
In the shell;
Snappity, crackity,
Out it fell!

Theme Connections

Seasons
Squirrels

Star Light, Star Bright

Star light, star bright,
First star I see tonight.
I wish I may, I wish I might
Have this wish I wish tonight.

Theme Connections

Sun, Moon, Stars
Time of Day

The Star-Spangled Banner
by Francis Scott Key

Oh, say, can you see, by the dawn's early light,
What so proudly we hailed at the twilight's last gleaming,
Whose broad stripes and bright stars, through the perilous
    fight,
O'er the ramparts we watched were so gallantly streaming?
And the rocket's red glare, the bombs bursting in air,
Gave proof through the night that our flag was still there.
Oh, say, does that Star Spangled Banner yet wave,
O'er the land of the free and the home of the brave?

Theme Connections

Holidays
Patriotism

Stop, Look, and Listen

Stop, look, and listen
Before you cross the street.
First use your eyes and ears,
Then use your feet.

Theme Connections

Health and Safety
Senses

Stretching Chant

(suit actions to words)
Stretch to the windows,
Stretch to the door,
Stretch up to the ceiling
And bend to the floor.

Theme Connections

Movement
Opposites
Spatial Relationships

Stretching Fun

I stretch and stretch and find it fun *(stretch)*
To try to reach up to the sun. *(reach hands up)*
I bend and bend to touch the ground, *(touch the ground)*
Then I twist and twist around. *(twist side to side)*

Theme Connections

Movement
Spatial Relationships

Sur le Pont d'Avignon

Sur le pont d'Avignon
L'on y danse, l'on y danse,
Sur le pont d'Avignon
L'on y danse tout en rond.

English Translation

On the bridge of Avignon
All are dancing, all are dancing
On the bridge of Avignon
All are dancing in a row.

Theme Connections

Languages
Movement

Susie Moriar

This is the story of Susie Moriar
It started one night as Susie sat by the _____. (fire)
The fire was so hot
Susie jumped in a _____. (pot)
The pot was so black
Susie dropped in a _____. (crack)
The crack was so narrow
She climbed in a wheel_____. (barrow)
The wheelbarrow was so low
Susie fell in the _____. (snow)
The snow was so white,
Susie stayed there all _____. (night)
The night was so long,
Susie sang a _____. (song)
The song was so sweet,
Susie ran down the _____. (street)
The street was so clean,
Susie picked up a _____. (bean)
The bean was so hard,
Susie dropped it in _____. (lard)
The lard was so greasy,
Susie nearly jumped _____. (fleecy)
And when she came down,
She ran through the _____. (town)
The town was so big,
Susie jumped on a _____. (pig)
The pig jumped so high,
He touched the _____. (sky)
He touched the sky
And he couldn't touch higher
But oh! What a ride
Had Susie _____. (Moriar)

Theme Connections

Humor
Sounds of Language

Swim Little Fishie

Swim little fishie
Swim around the pool.
Swim little fishie
The water is cool.
Where's the little fishie?
Where did he go?
There he is!
Splash!

Theme Connection

Fish

The Swing
by Robert Louis Stevenson

How do you like to go up in a swing,
Up in the air so blue?
Oh, I do think it the pleasantest thing
Ever a child can do!

Up in the air and over the wall,
Till I can see so wide,
River and trees and cattle and all
Over the countryside.

Theme Connections

Movement
Nature
Self-esteem

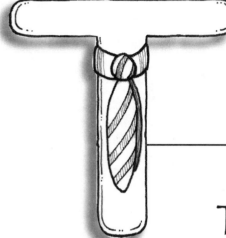

Take Me Out to the Ball Game

Take me out to the ball game
Take me out with the crowd.
Buy me some peanuts and crackerjack,
I don't care if I ever get back.
So it's root, root, root for the home team,
If they don't win it's a shame.
For it's one, two, three strikes
You're out! at the old ball game.

Theme Connections

Counting
Food

Taps

Day is done,
Gone the sun,
From the lake,
From the hill,
From the sky,
All is well, safely rest,
God is nigh.

Theme Connections

Naptime, Sleeping
Sun, Moon, Stars
Time of Day

Teacher, Teacher

Teacher, teacher made a mistake.
She sat down on a chocolate cake.
The cake was soft; teacher fell off.
Teacher, teacher made a mistake.

Theme Connections

Food
Humor
Occupations

Teddy Bear, Teddy Bear

(suit actions to words)

Teddy bear, teddy bear,
Turn around.
Teddy bear, teddy bear,
Touch the ground.
Teddy bear, teddy bear,
Touch your shoe.
Teddy bear, teddy bear,
Say how-di-do.
Teddy bear, teddy bear,
Go up the stairs.
Teddy bear, teddy bear,
Say your prayers.
Turn out the light.
Say good night.

Theme Connections

Movement
Naptime/Sleeping
Spatial Relationships
Teddy Bears
Time of Day

Teeter Totter

Teeter-totter, bread and water
I'll be the son and you be the daughter.
I'll eat the bread and you drink the water.

Theme Connections

Families   Food

Ten in the Bed

There were ten in the bed *(hold up ten fingers)*
And the little one said,
"Roll over! Roll over!" *(roll hand over hand)*
So they all rolled over
And one rolled out. *(hold up one finger)*

There were nine in the bed. . . *(repeat hand motions)*
…eight in the bed. . .
…seven in the bed. . .
…six in the bed. . .
…five in the bed. . .
…four in the bed. . .
…three in the bed. . .
…two in the bed. . .

There was one in the bed
And the little one said,
"Alone at last!" *(place head on hands as if sleeping)*

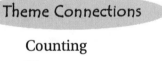

Theme Connections

Counting
Humor
Movement
Numbers

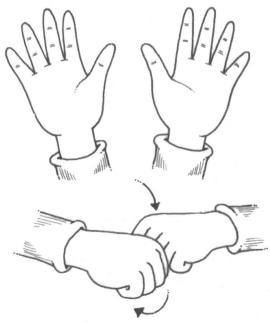

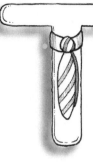

Ten Little Fingers

I have ten little fingers, *(hold up ten fingers)*
And they all belong to me. *(point to self)*
I can make them do things. *(wiggle fingers)*
Do you want to see? *(tilt head)*

I can make them point. *(point)*
I can make them hold. *(hold fingertips together)*
I can make them dance *(dance fingers on arm)*
And then I make them fold. *(fold hands in lap)*

Theme Connections

Parts of the Body
Self-esteem

Terrific Toes

I have such terrific toes
I take them with me wherever I goes.
I have such fantastic feet.
No matter what, they still smell sweet.
Toes and feet and feet and toes.
There's nothing else as fine as those.

Theme Connections

Humor
Parts of the Body
Self-esteem

Thank You

(suit actions to words)
My hands say thank you
With a clap, clap, clap.
My feet say thank you
With a tap, tap, tap.

Clap, clap, clap.
Tap, tap, tap.
I turn around,
Touch the ground,
And with a bow,
I say…Thank you, now.

Theme Connections

> Emotions
> Manners
> Parts of the Body

There Once Was a Queen

There once was a queen whose face was green,
She ate her milk and drank her bread
And got up in the morning to go to bed.

Theme Connections

> Food
> Humor
> Kings and Queens
> Opposites

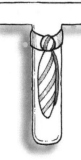

There Once Was a Sow

There once was a sow
Who had three piglets
And three piglets had she.
And the old sow always went "Umph,"
And the piglets went, "Wee, wee, wee."

Theme Connections

Animal Sounds
Pigs

There Once Was a Turtle

There was a little turtle. *(make a fist)*
He lived in a box. *(draw a square in the air)*
He swam in a puddle. *(pretend to swim)*
He climbed on the rocks. *(pretend to climb)*
He snapped at a mosquito. *(snap)*
He snapped at a flea. *(snap)*
He snapped at a minnow, *(snap)*
And he snapped at me. *(snap)*
He caught the mosquito. *(clap)*
He caught the flea. *(clap)*
He caught the minnow, *(clap)*
But he didn't catch me. *(wave index finger as if saying no-no)*

Theme Connections

Fish
Fleas

Mosquitoes
Nature

Turtles

There Was a Bee-Eye-Ee-Eye-Ee

There was a bee-eye-ee-eye-ee
Sat on a wall-eye-all-eye-all.
And there it sat-eye-at-eye-at
And that was all-eye-all-eye-all.

Then came a boy-eye-oy-eye-oy
Who had a stick-eye-ick-eye-ick.
And gave that bee-eye-ee-eye-ee
An awful lick-eye-ick-eye-ick.

And so that bee-eye-ee-eye-ee
Began to sting-eye-ing-eye-ing.
And hurt that boy-eye-oy-eye-oy
Like anything-eye-ing-eye-ing!

And then that bee-eye-ee-eye-ee
Gave one big cough-eye-off-eye-off.
And one last smile-eye-ile-eye-ile
And he buzzed off-eye-off-eye-off.

Theme Connections

Bees
Sounds of Language

There Was a Crooked Man

There was a crooked man who walked a crooked mile.
He found a crooked sixpence against a crooked stile.
He bought a crooked cat, which caught a crooked mouse.
And they all lived together in a little crooked house.

Theme Connections

Cats
Houses and Homes
Mice
Money

There Was a Little Boy

There was a little boy went into a barn
And lay down on some hay.
An owl came out and flew about,
And the little boy ran away.

Theme Connections

Emotions
Farms
Owls

There Was a Little Girl

There was a little girl, and she had a little curl
Right in the middle of her forehead.
When she was good, she was very, very good,
But when she was bad, she was horrid.

Theme Connections

Emotions

There Was a Maid on Scrabble Hill

There was a maid on Scrabble Hill,
And, if not dead, she lives there still.
She grew so tall, she reached the sky,
And on the moon hung clothes to dry.

Theme Connections

Humor
Sun, Moon, Stars

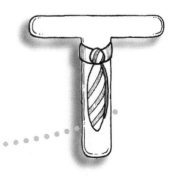

There Was an Old Lady Who Swallowed a Fly

I know an old lady who swallowed a fly
I don't know why she swallowed the fly
Perhaps she'll die.

I know an old lady who swallowed a spider
That wiggled and jiggled and tickled inside her.
She swallowed the spider to catch the fly,
But I don't know why she swallowed the fly.
Perhaps she'll die.

I know an old lady who swallowed a bird.
How absurd! She swallowed a bird.
She swallowed the bird to catch the spider
That wiggled and jiggled and tickled inside her,
She swallowed the spider to catch the fly,
But I don't know why she swallowed the fly.
Perhaps she'll die.

I know and old lady who swallowed a cat.
Think of that! She swallowed a cat.
She swallowed a cat to catch the bird.
She swallowed the bird to catch the spider,
That wiggled and jiggled and tickled inside her,
She swallowed the spider to catch the fly,
I don't know why she swallowed the fly.
Perhaps she'll die.

I know an old lady who swallowed a dog.
What a hog! She swallowed a dog.
She swallowed the dog to catch the cat,
She swallowed the cat to catch the bird,

She swallowed the bird to catch the spider,
That wiggled and jiggled and tickled inside her,
She swallowed the spider to catch the fly,
But I don't know why she swallowed the fly.
Perhaps she'll die.

I know and old lady who swallowed a goat.
It stuck in her throat! She swallowed a goat.
She swallowed the goat to catch the dog,
She swallowed the dog to catch the cat,
She swallowed the cat to catch the bird,
She swallowed the bird to catch the spider,
That wiggled and jiggled and tickled inside her,
She swallowed the spider to catch the fly,
But I don't know why she swallowed the fly.
Perhaps she'll die.

I know an old lady who swallowed a horse.
She's dead, of course!

Theme Connections

Birds
Cats
Dogs
Goats
Horses
Humor
Spiders

There Was an Old Woman, and What Do You Think?

There was an old woman, and what do you think?
She lived upon nothing but victuals and drink;
Victuals and drink were the chief of her diet,
And yet this old woman could never keep quiet.

Theme Connections

Food

There Was an Old Woman
(lived under some stairs)

There was an old woman lived under some stairs,
He, haw, haw, hum.
She sold apples and sold pears,
He, haw, haw, hum.
All her bright money she laid on the shelf,
He, haw, haw, hum.
If you want any more, you may sing it yourself,
He, haw, haw, hum.

Theme Connections

Food
Money

There Was an Old Woman
(tossed up in a basket)

There was an old woman tossed up in a basket
Seventeen times as high as the moon.
And where was she going, I couldn't but ask it.
For in her hand she carried a broom.
"Old woman, old woman, old woman," said I,
"Oh whither, oh whither, oh whither so high?"
To sweep the cobwebs off the sky."
"Shall I go with you?" "Aye, by and by."

Theme Connections

Sun, Moon, Stars

There Was an Old Woman
(who lived under a hill)

There was an old woman
Who lived under a hill,
And if she's not gone
She lives there still.

Theme Connections

Houses and Homes

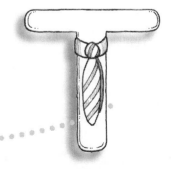

There Were Three Cooks of Colebrook

There were three cooks of Colebrook
And they fell out with our cook.
And all was for a pudding he took
From the three cooks of Colebrook.

Theme Connections

Cooking
Emotions
Food
Occupations

There Were Three Jovial Huntsmen

There were three jovial huntsmen,
As I have heard them say,
And they would go a-hunting
All on a summer's day.

All the day they hunted,
And nothing could they find
But a ship a-sailing,
A-sailing with the wind.

One said it was a ship,
The other he said nay;
The third said it was a house
With the chimney blown away.

And all the night they hunted,
And nothing could they find
But the moon a-gliding,
A-gliding with the wind.

One said it was the moon,
The other he said nay;
The third said it was a cheese,
And half o't cut away.

Theme Connections

Sun, Moon, Stars
Weather

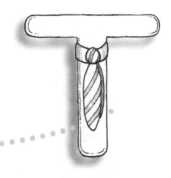

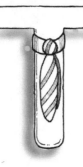

There's a Hole in the Middle of the Sea

There's a hole in the middle of the sea,
There's a hole in the middle of the sea,
There's a hole, there's a hole
There's a hole in the middle of the sea.

There's a log in the hole in the middle of the sea.
There's a log in the hole in the middle of the sea.
There's a log, there's a log
There's a log in the hole in the middle of the sea.

There's a bump on the log in the hole in the middle of
   the sea…
There's a frog on the bump on the log in the hole in the
   middle of the sea…
There's a fly on the frog on the bump on the log in the hole
   in the middle of the sea…
There's a wing on the fly on the frog on the bump on the log
   in the hole in the middle of the sea…
There's a flea on the wing on the fly on the frog on the
   bump on the log in the hole in the middle of the sea…

Theme Connections

Flies
Frogs
Oceans and Seas

There's a Hole in the Bucket

There's a hole in the bucket,
Dear Liza, dear Liza.
There's a hole in the bucket,
Dear Liza, there's a hole.

Then fix it, dear Henry,
Dear Henry, dear Henry.
Then fix it, dear Henry,
Dear Henry, fix it.

With what shall I fix it,
Dear Liza, dear Liza?
With what shall I fix it,
Dear Liza, with what?

With a straw, dear Henry,
Dear Henry, dear Henry.
With a straw, dear Henry,
Dear Henry, with a straw.

But the straw is too long,
Dear Liza, dear Liza.
But the straw is too long,
Dear Liza, too long.

Then cut it, dear Henry,
Dear Henry, dear Henry.
Then cut it, dear Henry,
Dear Henry, cut it.

With what shall I cut it,
Dear Liza, dear Liza?
With what shall I cut it,
Dear Liza, with what?

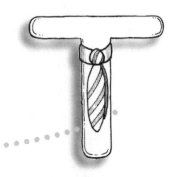

With an axe, dear Henry,
Dear Henry, dear Henry.
With an axe, dear Henry,
Dear Henry, an axe.

The axe is too dull,
Dear Liza, dear Liza.
The axe is too dull,
Dear Liza, too dull.

Then sharpen it, dear Henry,
Dear Henry, dear Henry.
Then sharpen it, dear Henry,
Dear Henry, sharpen it.

With what shall I sharpen it,
Dear Liza, dear Liza?
With what shall I sharpen it,
Dear Liza, with what?

With a stone, dear Henry,
Dear Henry, dear Henry.
With a stone, dear Henry,
Dear Henry, a stone.

The stone is too dry,
Dear Liza, dear Liza.
The stone is too dry,
Dear Liza, too dry.

Then whet it, dear Henry,
Dear Henry, dear Henry.
Then whet it, dear Henry,
Dear Henry, wet it.

With what shall I whet it,
Dear Liza, dear Liza?
With what shall I whet it,
Dear Liza, with what?

With water, dear Henry,
Dear Henry, dear Henry.
With water, dear Henry,
Dear Henry, with water.

How shall I get it,
Dear Liza, dear Liza?
How shall I get it,
Dear Liza, get it?

In the bucket, dear Henry,
Dear Henry, dear Henry.
In the bucket, dear Henry,
Dear Henry, in the bucket.

There's a hole in the bucket…

Theme Connections

Friends
Humor

These Are Mother's Knives and Forks

These are Mother's knives and forks. *(interlock as in praying fingers and lift them slightly)*
And this is our dining table. *(lower fingers keeping them interlocked, straighten wrist to form a flat surface)*
This is Sister's looking glass. *(form a circle with thumb and index finger)*
And this is the baby's cradle. *(cup hand together to form cradle)*

Theme Connections

Babies
Families

They That Wash on Monday

They that wash on Monday,
Have all the week to dry.
They that wash on Tuesday,
Are not so much awry.
They that wash on Wednesday,
Are not so much to blame.
They that wash on Thursday,
Wash for very shame.
They that wash on Friday,
Wash in sorry need.
They that wash on Saturday
Are lazy folk indeed.

Theme Connections

Days of the Week
Work

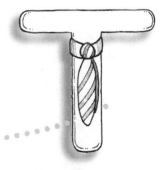

Thirty Days Hath September

Thirty days hath September,
April, June, and November;
All the rest have thirty-one,
Excepting February alone,
And that has twenty-eight days clear
And twenty-nine in each leap year.

Theme Connections

Months of the Year
Numbers

This Is the Church

This is the church, *(hold hands down with fingers interlocked)*
This is the steeple. *(raise both index fingers)*
Look inside. *(turn hands over)*
And see all the people. *(wiggle fingers)*

Theme Connections

Neighborhoods

This Is the Way We Wash Our Face

(Tune: Mulberry Bush)

This is the way we wash our face,
Scrub our cheeks,
Scrub our ears,
This is the way we wash our face,
Until we're squeaky clean.

Theme Connections

Health and Safety
Parts of the Body
Self-esteem

This Little Doggie

This little doggie ran away to play.
This little doggie said, "I'll go, too, someday."
This little doggie began to dig and dig.
This little doggie danced a funny jig.
This little doggie cried "ki yi ki yi, I wish I were big."

Hold up fingers of one hand and point to each finger as you say the rhyme.

Theme Connections

Dogs
Opposites

This Little Finger

This little finger holds on tight. *(wiggle each finger as it is mentioned)*
This little finger points just right.
This little finger helps wave bye-bye.
This little finger wipes my eye.
This little finger holds, points, waves, and wipes.
Sweet little hands hold on tight.

Theme Connections

Parts of the Body

This Little Hand

This little hand
   (hold up one hand)
This little hand is his brother
   (hold up other hand)
Together, they wash and they wash and they wash.
   (wash hands)
One hand washes the other.

Theme Connections

Parts of the Body
Health and Safety

This Little Light of Mine

This little light of mine,
I'm going to let it shine.
This little light of mine,
I'm going to let it shine.
This little light of mine,
I'm going to let it shine.
Ev'ry day, ev'ry day,
Ev'ry day, ev'ry day,
Gonna let my little light shine.

Theme Connections

Self-esteem

This Little Pig

This little pig said, "I want some corn."
This little pig said, "Where are you going to get it?"
This little pig said, "Out of Master's barn."
This little pig said, "I'll go and tell."
And this little pig said,"Queeky, queeky,
I can't get over the barn door sill."

Theme Connections

Animal Sounds
Farms
Food
Pigs

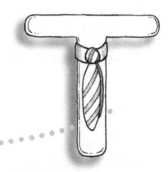

This Little Piggy

This little piggy went to market, *(wiggle big toe or finger)*
This little piggy stayed home, *(wiggle second toe)*
This little piggy had roast beef, *(wiggle middle toe)*
This little piggy had none, *(wiggle fourth toe)*
And this little piggy cried
"Wee-wee-wee!" all the way home. *(wiggle little toe)*

Theme Connections

Houses and Homes
Parts of the Body
Pigs
Movement

This Little Snail

The snail is so slow, the snail is so slow.
He creeps and creeps along.
The snail is so-o-o s-l-o-w.

Theme Connections

Snails

This Old Man

This old man, he played one. *(hold up one finger)*
He played knick-knack on my thumb. *(knock on thumb)*

Chorus:
With a knick-knack paddy whack give a dog a bone. *(knock on head, clap twice, pretend to throw a bone over your shoulder)*
This old man came rolling home. *(roll hand over hand)*

This old man, he played two. *(hold up two fingers)*
He played knick-knack on my shoe. *(knock on shoe)*

Chorus

This old man, he played three. *(hold up three fingers)*
He played knick-knack on my knee. *(knock on knee)*

Chorus

This old man, he played four. *(hold up four fingers)*
He played knick-knack on the door. *(pretend to knock on door)*

Chorus

This old man, he played five. *(hold up five fingers)*
He played knick-knack on a hive. *(pretend to knock on a hive)*

Chorus

…six…sticks *(continue hand motions)*
…seven…heaven
…eight…gate
…nine…line
…ten…over again!

Theme Connections

Counting
Numbers

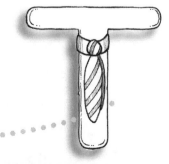

Three Jolly Gentlemen

Three jolly gentlemen
In coats of red
Rode their horses
Up to bed.

Three jolly gentlemen
Snored till morn,
Their horses chomping
The golden corn.

Three jolly gentlemen
At break of day,
Came clitter-clatter down the stairs
And galloped away.

Theme Connections

Colors
Horses
Numbers
Time of Day

Three Little Kittens

Three little kittens lost their mittens;
And they began to cry,
"Oh, mother dear, we very much fear
our mittens we have lost."

"What! lost your mittens, you naughty kittens!
Then you shall have no pie."
"Mee-ow, mee-ow, mee-ow, mee-ow."
"No, you shall have no pie."

The three little kittens they found their mittens;
And they began to cry,
"Oh, Mother dear, see here, see here!
Our mittens we have found."

"What! Found your mittens! You good little kittens,
Now you shall have some pie."
"Purr, purr, purr, purr,
Purr, purr, purr."

Theme Connections

Cats
Emotions
Families
Food

Three Little Witches

One little, two little, three little witches,
Fly over haystacks, fly over ditches,
Slide down the moon without any hitches.
Hey ho, Halloween's here!

Theme Connections

Counting
Holidays
Sun, Moon, Stars

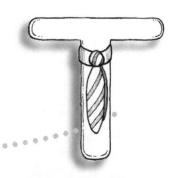

Three Men in a Tub

Rub-a-dub-dub, three men in a tub,
And who do you think were there?
The butcher, the baker, the candlestick-maker,
And all had come from the fair.

Variation

Rub-a-dub-dub,
Three men in a tub—-
And who do you think they be?
The butcher, the baker,
The candlestick maker—-
Turn 'em out,
Knaves all three!

Rub-a-dub-dub
Three men in a tub,
And how do you think they got there?
The butcher, the baker, the candlestick-maker —
They all jumped out of a rotten potato!
'Twas enough to make a fish stare.

Theme Connections

Numbers
Occupations

Three Wise Men of Gotham

Three wise men of Gotham
Went to sea in a bowl;
If the bowl had been stronger,
My song would have been longer.

Theme Connections

Numbers
Oceans and Seas

Thumbkin, Pointer

Thumbkin, Pointer, Middleman big, *(point to each finger)*
Silly Man, Wee Man,
Rig-a-jig-jig. *(roll hands around each other)*

Theme Connection

Parts of the Body

A Thunderstorm

Boom, bang, boom, bang,
Rumpety, lumpety, bump!
Zoom, zam, zoom, zam,
Clippity, clappity, clump!
Rustles and bustles,
And swishes and zings!
What wonderful sounds
A thunderstorm brings.

Theme Connections

Sounds of Language
Weather

Tidy Up

Tidy up,
Tidy up,
Everybody tidy up
Right now.

Theme Connections

Cleanup
Toys

Time to Pick Up

Now it is time
To end our day.
Pick up our toys
And put them away.

Theme Connections

Cleanup
Toys

Tiny Seeds

Tiny seed planted just right, *(tuck into a ball)*
Not a breath of air, not a ray of light.
Rain falls slowly to and fro,
And now the seed begins to grow. *(begin to unfold)*
Slowly reaching for the light,
With all its energy, all its might.
The little seed's work is almost done,
To grow up tall and face the sun. *(stand up tall with arms
    stretched out)*

Theme Connections

Growing Things
Nature
Sun, Moon, Stars
Weather

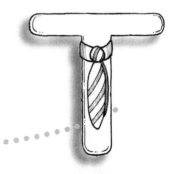

Tiny Tim

I had a little turtle,
His name was Tiny Tim.
I put him in the bathtub,
To see if he could swim.

He drank up all the water,
He ate up all the soap,
Tiny Tim was choking
On the bubbles in his throat.

In came the doctor,
In came the nurse,
In came the lady,
With the alligator purse.

They pumped out all the water,
They pumped out all the soap,
They popped the airy bubbles
As they floated from his throat.

Out went the doctor,
Out went the nurse,
Out went the lady
With the alligator purse.

Theme Connections

Humor
Occupations
Turtles

Variation

Mother, Mother, I am ill;
Call the doctor from over the hill.
In came the doctor, in came the nurse,
In came the lady with the alligator purse.
"Measles," said the doctor.
"Mumps," said the nurse.
"Nothing," said the lady with the alligator purse.

Tippety Tin

Tippety, tippety, tippety tin
Give me a kiss and I'll come in.
Tippety, tippety, tippety toe
Give me a kiss and I will go.
Tippety, tippety, tippety tin
Give me a pancake and I'll come in.
Tippety, tippety, tippety toe
Give me a pancake and I will go.

Change the words to fit any subject matter.

Theme Connections

Food
Opposites
Sounds

A Tisket, A Tasket

A tisket, a tasket,
A green and yellow basket,
I wrote a letter to my love
And on the way I lost it.

I lost it, I lost it,
And on the way I lost it.
A little boy, he picked it up,
And put it in his pocket.

Theme Connections

Colors
Emotions

His pocket, his pocket,
He put it in his pocket.
A little boy, he picked it up,
And put it in his pocket.

To Market, to Market

To market, to market,
To buy a fat pig.
Home again, home again,
Jiggety-jig.

To market, to market,
To buy a fat hog.
Home again, home again,
Jiggety-jog.

Variation

To market, to market, to buy a fat pig,
Home again, home again, jiggety jig.
To market, to market, to buy a fat hog,
Home again, home again, jiggety jog.
To market, to market, to buy a plum bun,
Home again, home again, marketing's done.

Theme Connections

Houses and Homes
Pigs

Today Is a Birthday!

Today is a birthday
I wonder for whom.
We know it's somebody
Who's right in this room.
So look all around you
For somebody who
Is laughing and smiling
My goodness—it's you!

Happy Birthday, _____
From all of us to you.
Happy Birthday, _____
From Mommy and Daddy, too.
We congratulate you,
With all good wishes for you!
Happy Birthday, _____
May all of your good dreams come true!

Theme Connections

Birthdays
Celebrations
Families

Tom, Tom

Tom, Tom, the piper's son,
Stole a pig*, and away he run!
The pig was eat, and Tom was beat,
   And Tom went roaring down the street.

*A pig is a currant bun made in the shape of a pig.

Theme Connections

Emotions
Families
Food

Tommy Thumbs

Tommy Thumbs up and *(thumbs up sign)*
Tommy Thumbs down. *(both thumbs down)*
Tommy Thumbs dancing *(dance thumbs)*
All around the town.
Dance 'em on your shoulders. *(bounce them on shoulders)*
Dance 'em on your head. *(dance thumbs on head)*
Dance 'em on your knees. *(dance thumbs on knees)*
Tuck them into bed. *(fold arms, hiding hands)*

Peter Pointer up…
Toby Tall up…
Ring man up…
Baby Finger up…
Finger Family up…

Theme Connections

Movement
Opposites
Parts of the Body

Tooty Ta

(suit actions to words)
Tooty ta, tooty ta,
tooty ta, ta.

Thumbs up
Tooty ta, tooty ta,
tooty ta, ta.

Elbows back
Tooty ta, tooty ta,
Tooty ta, ta.

Feet apart
Tooty ta, tooty ta,
Tooty ta, ta.

Knees together
Tooty ta, tooty ta,
Tooty ta, ta.

Bottoms up
Tooty ta, tooty ta,
Tooty ta, ta.

Tongue out
Tooty ta, tooty ta,
Tooty ta, ta.

Eyes shut
Tooty ta, tooty ta,
Tooty ta, ta.

Turn around
Tooty ta, tooty ta,
Tooty ta, ta.

Beginning consonants can be changed to any letter—"Tooty ta" can be "mooty ma," etc.

Theme Connections

Movement
Parts of the Body
Sounds of Language

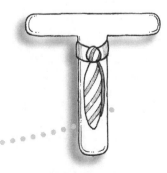

Toys Away

Toys away, toys away, *(chant two or three times)*
Time to put your _____ away. *(name a toy)*

Theme Connections

Cleanup
Toys

The Turtle

The turtle crawls on the ground
And makes a rustling sound.
He carries his house wherever he goes,
And when he is scared,
He pulls in his nose and covers his toes!

Theme Connections

Emotions
Houses and Homes
Turtles

Twenty White Horses

Twenty white horses
Upon a red hill;
Now they tramp,
Now they chomp,
Now they stand still.
(A child's teeth)

Variation

Thirty-two white horses on a red hill,
When you say "stop," they all stand still.
(teeth)

Theme Connections

Horses
Humor
Parts of the Body

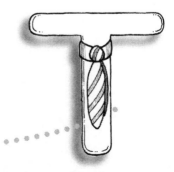

Twinkle, Twinkle, Little Star

Twinkle, twinkle, little star,
How I wonder what you are!
Up above the world so high,
Like a diamond in the sky.

When the blazing sun is set,
And the grass with dew is wet,
Then you show your little light,
Twinkle, twinkle, all the night.

Then the traveler in the dark
Thanks you for your tiny spark.
How could he see where to go
If you did not twinkle so?

In the dark-blue sky you keep,
And often through my curtains peep.
For you never shut an eye
Till the sun is in the sky.

As your bright and tiny spark
Lights the traveler in the dark,
Though I know not what you are,
Twinkle, twinkle, little star.

Theme Connections

Sun, Moon, Stars
Time of Day

A Twister of Twists

A twister of twists once twisted a twist,
The twist that he twisted was a three-twisted twist;
If in twisting the twist, one twist should untwist,
The untwisted twist would untwist the twist.

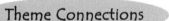

Theme Connections

Sounds of Language

Two Crows

There were two crows sat on a stone,
Fal de ral, fal de ral.
One flew away and there was one,
Fal de ral, fal de ral.
The other seeing his neighbour gone,
Fal de ral, fal de ral.
He flew away and then there were none,
Fal de ral, fal de ral.

Theme Connections

Birds
Counting
Numbers

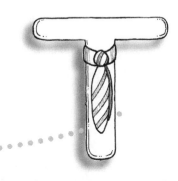

Two in the Middle

Two in the middle and two at the end,
Each is a sister and each is a friend.
A penny to save and a penny to spend,
Two in the middle and two at the end.

Theme Connections

Families
Friends
Money
Numbers

Two Little Blackbirds

Two little blackbirds *(hold up index finger of each hand)*
Sitting on a hill.
One named Jack. *(hold right hand/finger forward)*
One named Jill. *(hold left hand/finger forward)*
Fly away, Jack. *(wiggle right finger and place behind your back)*
Fly away, Jill. *(wiggle left finger and place behind your back)*
Come back, Jack. *(bring right hand back)*
Come back, Jill. *(bring left hand back)*

Theme Connections

Birds
Colors
Opposites

Two Little Dogs

Two little dogs sat by the fire
In a basket of coal dust.
Says one little dog to the other little dog,
If you don't speak then I must.

Theme Connections

Dogs

Two Little Houses

Two little houses,
Closed up tight. *(close fists)*
Let's open the windows,
And let in some light. *(open fists)*

Theme Connections

Houses and Homes

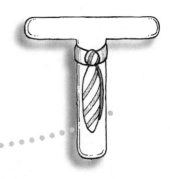

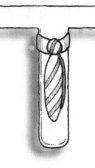

Two Sticks and an Apple

Two sticks and an apple,
Say the bells at Whitechapel.
Old Father Baldgate,
Say the slow bells at Aldgate.
Maids in white aprons,
Say the bells at St. Catherine's.
Oranges and lemons,
Say the bells at St. Clement's.

Theme Connections

Apples
Colors
Humor

Un, Deux, Trois

Un, deux, trois, quatre, cinq, six, sept
  (show number of fingers)
Violettes, violettes.
Un, deux, trois, quatre, cinq, six, sept
A bicyclette, a bicyclette. *(roll hands around)*

Theme Connections

Counting
Languages
Numbers

Under the Spreading Chestnut Tree

Under the spreading chestnut tree
There I held her on my knee.
We were happy yesiree.
Under the spreading chestnut tree.

Theme Connections

Emotions
Nature

Uno, dos, y tres

Uno, dos, y tres,
Cuatro, sinco, seis.
Siete, ocho, nueve,
Cuento hasta diez.
La la la la la; La la la la la,
La la la la la; La la la la la.
La la la la la; La la la la la.

Theme Connections

Counting
Languages

English Translation

One, two, and three,
Four, five, and six.
Seven, eight, nine,
I can count to ten.
La la la la la; La la la la la,
La la la la la; La la la la la.
La la la la la; La la la la la.

A bilingual counting song in Spanish and English.

Unwind the Thread

Unwind, wind the thread.
Unwind, wind the thread.
Pull the thread, pull the thread.
Clap, clap, clap.

Rotate arms one around the other, first outward, then at
"wind," inward towards the body; on the third and fourth
lines pull the "thread" and clap.

Theme Connections

Movement
Work

Up in the Green Orchard

Up in the green orchard there is a green tree
The finest of pippins that you may see.
The apples are ripe and ready to fall
And Robin and Richard shall gather them all.

Theme Connections

Apples
Colors
Food

Up the Wooden Hill

Up the wooden hill to Blanket Fair,
What shall we have when we get there?
A bucket full of water,
And a pennyworth of hay,
Gee up, Dobbin,
All the way.

Theme Connections

Horses
Money
Nature

Up to the Ceiling

Up to the ceiling, *(raise hands up)*
Down to the floor, *(put hands down)*
Left to the window, *(point left with the left hand)*
Right to the door. *(point right with the right hand)*
This is my right hand—
Raise it up high. *(raise right hand)*
This is my left hand—
Reach for the sky. *(raise left hand up, keep right up)*
Right hand, left hand,
Twirl them around. *(twirl hands one over another)*
Left hand, right hand,
Pound, pound, pound. *(hit fists on on the other)*

Theme Connections

Movement
Opposites

Upstairs, Downstairs

Upstairs, downstairs, upon my lady's window,
There I saw a cup of sack and a race of ginger,
Apples at the fire and nuts to crack,
And a little boy in the cream pot up to his neck.

Theme Connections

Apples
Food
Houses and Homes
Opposites

Vintery, Mintery, Cutery, Corn

Vintery, mintery, cutery, corn,
Apple seed and apple thorn;
Wire, briar, limber lock,
Three geese in a flock.
One flew east,
And one flew west,
And one flew over the cuckoo's nest.

Theme Connections

Apples
Geese
Opposites

Wake Up, Jack-in-the-Box

Jack-in-the-box, jack-in-the-box, *(suit actions to words)*
Wake up, wake up, somebody knocks.
One time, two times, three times, four.
Jack pops out of his little round door.

Theme Connections

Counting
Numbers
Opposites
Toys

Wake up, Jacob

Wake up, Jacob *(or any name)*, day's a-breakin',
Peas in the pot and pancakes bakin',
Bacon's in the pan and coffee's in the pot;
Come on round and get it while it's hot.
(shout) WAKE SNAKES AND BITE A BISCUIT.

Theme Connections

Food
Time of Day

A Walk One Day

When I went out for a walk one day
My head fell off and rolled away,
And when I saw that it was gone
I picked it up and put it on.

When I went into the street
Someone shouted, "Look at your feet."
I looked at them and sadly said
I've left them both asleep in bed.

Theme Connections

Humor
Parts of the Body

Warm Hands

Warm hands, warm,
The men are gone to plow.
If you want to warm your hands,
Warm your hands now.

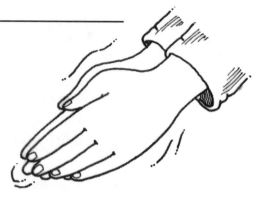

Variation

Warm hands, warm, *(put hands together)*
Do you know how? *(clap gently)*
If you want to warm your hands,
Warm you hands now. *(rub your hands)*

Theme Connections

Farms
Movement
Parts of the Body

Wash the Dishes

Wash the dishes,
Wipe the dishes,
Ring the bell for tea.
Three good wishes,
Three good kisses,
I will give to thee.

Theme Connections

Counting
Emotions
Numbers
Work

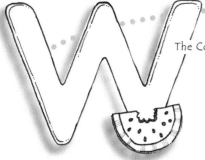

Way Down South

Way down south where bananas grow,
A fly stepped on an elephant's toe.
The elephant cried with tears in his eyes,
"Why don't you pick on someone your own size?"

I asked my mother for fifty cents
To see the elephant jump a fence.
He jumped so high, he reached the sky,
And didn't get down 'til the Fourth of July.

I asked my mother for fifty more
To see the elephant scrub the floor.
He scrubbed so slow he stubbed his toe,
And that was the end of the elephant show.

Theme Connections

Elephants
Holidays
Humor
Money

Way Down Yonder

Way down yonder a little ways off,
A jaybird died from the whooping cough.
He whooped so hard with the whooping cough,
He whooped his head and tail right off.

Variation

Up in the north a long way off,
A donkey caught the whooping cough.

What shall we give him to make him better?
Salt, mustard, vinegar, and pepper.

Up in the north a long way off,
The donkey's got the whooping cough.
He whooped so hard with the whooping cough,
He whooped his head and his tail right off.

Theme Connections

Birds
Humor

We Can

(suit actions to words)
We can jump, jump, jump,
We can hop, hop, hop,
We can clap, clap, clap,
We can stop, stop, stop.

We can nod our heads for yes,
We can shake our heads for no.
We can bend our knees a tiny bit,
And sit down slow.

Theme Connections

Movement
Parts of the Body
Self-esteem

We Wish You a Merry Christmas

We wish you a Merry Christmas,
We wish you a Merry Christmas,
We wish you a Merry Christmas,
And a Happy New Year!

Good tidings to you, wherever you are;
Good tidings, Merry Christmas,
And a Happy New Year.

Theme Connection

Holidays

Wee Willie Winkie

Wee Willie Winkie runs through the town,
Upstairs and downstairs in his nightgown,
Rapping at the window, crying through the lock,
"Are the children in their beds, for now it's eight o'clock?"

Theme Connections

Naptime/Sleeping
Opposites
Time of Day

What Do You See?

What do you see? A pig in a tree.
Where's your cat? Under my hat.
How do you know? He licked my toe.

Theme Connections

Cats
Humor
Pigs

What the Animals Say

Little pup, little pup,
What do you say?
"Woof, woof, woof!
Let's go and play."

Kittycat, kittycat,
How about you?
"Meow, meow, meow!
And I purr, too."

Pretty bird, pretty bird,
Have you a song?
"Tweet, tweet, tweet!
The whole day long."

Jersey cow, Jersey cow,
What do you do?
"Moo, moo, moo!
And give milk, too."

Little lamb, little lamb,
What do you say?
"Baa, baa, baa!
Can Mary play?"

Theme Connections

Animal Sounds   Cows
Birds   Puppies
Cats   Sheep

WOOF

What'll I Do With My Baby-O?

What'll I do with my baby-o?
What'll I do with my baby-o?
What'll I do with my baby-o?
If she won't go to sleep-o?

Wrap her up in calico,
Wrap her up in calico,
Wrap her up in calico,
And send her to her daddy-o (or mammy-o).

Theme Connections

Babies
Families
Naptime/Sleeping

Wheels on the Bus

The wheels on the bus go round and round. *(move hands in circular motion)*
Round and round, round and round.
The wheels on the bus go round and round,
All around the town. *(extend arms up and out)*

The windshield wipers go swish, swish, swish. *(sway hands back and forth)*
The baby on the bus goes, "Wah, wah, wah." *(rub eyes)*

People on the bus go up and down *(stand up, sit down)*
The horn on the bus goes beep, beep, beep. *(pretend to beep horn)*
The money on the bus goes clink, clink, clink. *(drop change in)*
The driver on the bus says, "Move on back." *(hitchhiking movement)*

Theme Connections

Occupations
Sounds of Language
Transportation

When Ducks Get Up in the Morning

When ducks get up in the morning
They always say "Quack, Quack."
When ducks get up in the morning
They always say, "Quack, quack,"
Quack, quack, quack, quack, quack, quack."
They always say, "Quack, quack."

Other verses:
Birds—tweet
Cows—moo
Cats—meow

Theme Connections

Animal Sounds
Birds
Cats
Cows
Ducks

When I Was One

When I was one I was so small, *(hold up one finger)*
I could not speak a word at all. *(shake head)*
When I was two, I learned to talk. *(hold up two fingers)*
I learned to sing, I learned to walk. *(point to mouth and feet)*
When I was three, I grew and grew. *(hold up two fingers)*
Now I am four and so are you! *(hold up four fingers)*

Theme Connections

Celebrations
Counting
Growing Up
Numbers

When I Was Young

When I was young I had no sense.
I bought a fiddle for 50 cents.
The only tune I could play
Was "Over the Hills and Far Away."

So early in the morning,
So early in the morning,
So early in the morning,
Before the break of day.

Theme Connections

Money
Morning
Music
Time of Day

When Jack's a Very Good Boy

When Jack's a very good boy,
He shall have cakes and custard;
But when he does nothing but cry,
He shall have nothing but mustard.

Theme Connections

> Emotions
> Food

When That I Was But a Little Tiny Boy

When that I was but a little tiny boy,
With a hey, ho, the wind and the rain,
A foolish thing was but a toy,
And the rain it raineth every day.
With a hey, ho, the wind and the rain,
A foolish thing was but a toy.

Theme Connections

> Growing Up
> Toys
> Weather

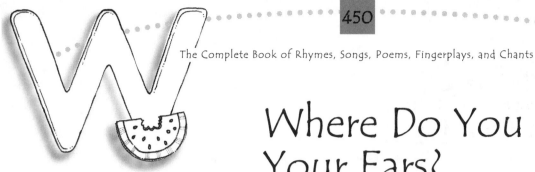

Where Do You Wear Your Ears?

Where do you wear your ears?
Underneath your hat?
Where do you wear your ears?
Yes ma'am, just like that.
Where do you wear your ears?
Say where, you sweet, sweet child.
Where do you wear your ears?
On both ends of my smile!

Theme Connections

Humor
Parts of the Body

Where Is Thumbkin?
(Tune: "Frere Jacques")

Where is thumbkin? *(hands behind back)*
Where is thumbkin?
Here I am. Here I am. *(bring out right thumb, then left)*
How are you today, sir? *(bend right thumb)*
Very well, I thank you. *(bend left thumb)*
Run away. Run away. *(put right thumb behind back, then
   left thumb behind back)*

Other verses:
Where is Pointer?
Where is Middle One?
Where is Ring Finger?
Where is Pinky?
Where are all of them?

Pulgarcito, donde estas

Pulgarcito, donde estas?

Pulgarcito, donde estas?

Aqui estoy! Aqui estoy!

Como esta usted? Muy bien, gracias!

Ya me voy. Ya me voy.

Indice, donde estas?…

Medio, donde estas?…

Anular, donde estas?…

Menique, donde esats?…

Mano, donde estas?…

Theme Connection

Parts of the Body

Where, Oh, Where Has My Little Dog Gone?

Where, oh, where has my little dog gone?

Where, oh, where can he be?

With his ears cut short and his tail cut long,

Oh, where, oh, where can he be?

Theme Connections

Dogs

Emotions

Whether the Weather

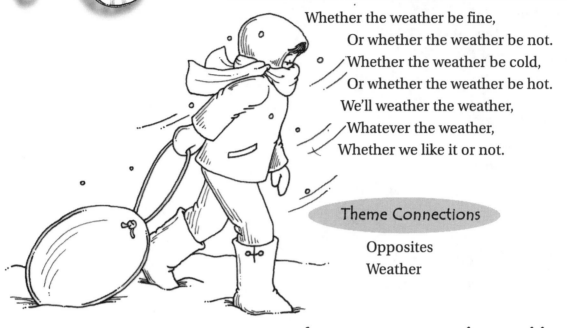

Whether the weather be fine,
Or whether the weather be not.
Whether the weather be cold,
Or whether the weather be hot.
We'll weather the weather,
Whatever the weather,
Whether we like it or not.

Theme Connections

Opposites
Weather

White Coral Bells

White coral bells upon a slender stalk,
Lilies of the Valley deck my garden walk.
Oh, don't you wish that you could hear them ring?
That will happen only when the fairies sing.

Theme Connections

Colors
Flowers
Nature

Who Is That Singing?

Who is that singing up in the chimney?
Who is that whistling through the bare trees?
That is the wind who flies as he listeth*,
That is the wind whom nobody sees.

Theme Connection

Weather

* Listeth means to choose or please.

Who Stole the Cookies from the Cookie Jar?

Group: Who stole the cookies from the cookie jar?
(Jimmy) stole the cookies from the cookie jar.
Jimmy: Who me?
Group: Yes, you!
Jimmy: Not me!
Group: Then who?
Jimmy: Linda stole the cookies from the cookie jar.
Linda: Who me?
Group: Yes, you!
(And so on)

Theme Connections

Food
Humor

A group of children forms a circle. Decide who will be called first or use a choosing rhyme (Eeeny, Meeny…). The group asks the question and answers it with the child's name. The child says, "Not me!" The group asks again. The child responds the same way. The group then asks who. The child gives the name of someone else in the group, and this chanting game continues.

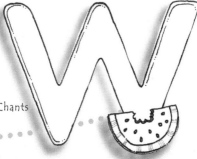

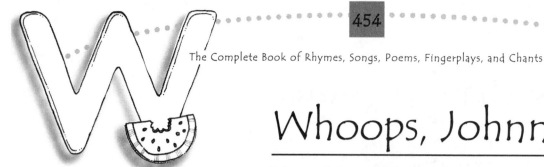

Whoops, Johnny

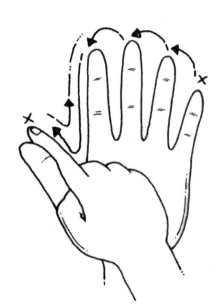

Johnny, Johnny, Johnny, Johnny,
Whoops, Johnny,
Whoops, Johnny,
Johnny, Johnny, Johnny, Johnny.

Tap the top of each finger, beginning with the pinky of the opposite hand. Say "Johnny" while tapping the top of each finger. Then slide the right index finger from the top of the left index finger down along the curve to the thumb, saying "Whoops," then "Johnny" at the top of the thumb. Repeat backwards to the pinky.

Theme Connections

Humor
Parts of the Body

Whose Little Pigs

Whose little pigs are these, these, these?
Whose little pigs are these?
They are Roger the cook's;
I know by their looks.
I found them among my peas.

Theme Connections

Farms
Pigs

Willoby Walloby Woo

Willaby, Walloby Woo
An elephant stepped on you
Willaby Walloby wee
An elephant stepped on me

Note: End the last "W" word to rhyme with any word. For example:
Willaby Walloby Wackie
An elephant stepped on Jackie.

Theme Connections

Elephants
Humor
Sounds of Language

Willy Boy, Willy Boy, Where Are You Going?

Willy boy, Willy boy, where are you going?
I'll go with you, if I may.
"I'm going to the meadow to see them a-mowing,
I'm going to help them make hay."

Theme Connections

Farms
Work

The Wind

I can blow like the wind. *(blow gently)*
I can bring the rain. *(move your fingers like falling rain drops)*
When I blow very softly, I can whisper my name. *(whisper child's name)*

Theme Connections

Movement
Opposites
Self-esteem
Weather

The Wind
(blows high)

The wind, the wind, the wind blows high.
The rain comes scattering down the sky.

Theme Connection

Weather

The Wind
(swoosh, swirl)

Swoosh, swirl, swoosh, swirl,
Watch the leaves tumble and twirl.

Theme Connections

Seasons
Sounds of Language
Weather

Wind the Bobbin

Wind, wind, wind the bobbin, *(roll hands)*
Wind, wind wind, the bobbin,
Pull, pull, Clap! Clap! Clap! *(pull arms out and clap)*

Theme Connections

Movement
Work

Window Watching

See the window I have here,

So big and wide and square. *(draw a square in the air)*

I can stand in front of it,

And see the things out there. *(shade eyes as if looking in the distance)*

Theme Connection

Senses

Windshield Wiper

I'm a windshield wiper. *(bend arm at elbow with fingers pointing up)*
This is how I go. *(move arm to left and right, pivoting at elbow)*
Back and forth, back and forth, *(continue back and forth motion)*
In the rain and snow. *(continue back and forth motion)*

Theme Connections

Movement
Opposites
Transportation
Weather

Wine and Cakes for Gentlemen

Wine and cakes for gentlemen,
Hay and corn for horses,
A cup of ale for good old wives,
And kisses for young lasses.

Theme Connections

Emotions
Food
Horses

Wynken, Blynken, and Nod

by Eugene Field

Wynken, Blynken, and Nod one night
Sailed off in a wooden shoe.
Sailed on a river of crystal light
Into a sea of dew.
"Where are you going, and what do you wish?"
The old moon asked the three.
"We have come to fish for the herring fish
That live in this beautiful sea.
Nets of silver and gold have we!"
Said Wynken,
Blynken,
And Nod.

The old moon laughed and sang a song,
As they rocked in the wooden shoe,
And the wind that sped them all night long,
Ruffled the waves of dew.
The little stars were the herring fish
That lived in that beautiful sea.
"Now cast your nets wherever you wish—
Never afeared are we."
So cried the stars to the fisherman three:
Wynken,
Blyken,
And Nod.

All night long their nets they threw
To the stars in the twinkling foam;
Then down from the skies came the wooden shoe,
Bringing the fisherman home.
'Twas all so pretty a sail it seemed
As if it could not be,
And some folks thought 'twas a dream they'd dreamed
Of sailing that beautiful sea;
But I shall name you the fisherman three:
Wynken,
Blynken,
And Nod.

Wynken and Blyken are two little eyes,
And Nod is a little head;
And the wooden shoe that sailed the skies
Is a wee one's trundle-bed.
So shut your eyes while mother sings
Of wonderful sights that be,
And you shall see the beautiful things
As you rock in the misty sea,
Where the old shoe rocked the fisherman three:
Wynken,
Blyken,
And Nod.

Theme Connections

Boats and Ships
Counting
Fish
Naptime/Sleeping
Numbers
Rivers
Sun, Moon, Stars
Time of Day

X, Y, and Tumbledown Z

X, Y, and tumbledown Z
The cat's in the cupboard,
And can't see me.

Variation

A, B, C, tumble down D.
The cat's in the cupboard
And can't see me.

Theme Connections

Alphabet
Cats

Yankee Doodle

Yankee Doodle came to town
Riding on a pony.
He stuck a feather in his cap
And called it macaroni.

Father and I went down to camp
Along with Captain Gooding,
And there we saw the men and boys
As thick as hasty pudding.

Yankee Doodle, keep it up
Yankee Doodle dandy,
Mind the music and the step
And with the girls be handy.

There was Captain Washington
Upon a slapping stallion,
A-giving orders to his men
I guess there was a million.

Yankee Doodle, keep it up
Yankee Doodle dandy.
Mind the music and the step
And with the girls be handy.

Theme Connections

Holidays
Horses
Patriotism

Yellow Rose of Texas

There's a yellow rose in Texas
I'm goin' back to see.
No other cowboy loves her
Half as much as me.

She cried so when I left her
It almost broke my heart.
And if we ever meet again
We'll never drift apart.

She's the sweetest rose of color
That Texas ever knew.
Her eyes are like the diamonds
They sparkle like the dew.

You can talk about your Clementine,
And dream of Rosalie,
But the Yellow Rose of Texas
Is the only girl for me.

Theme Connections

Cowboys and Cowgirls
Emotions
Flowers

Yorkshire Lullabye

Rock-a-boo baby, baby is bonny,
Two in a cradle, three is too many.
Four is a company, five is a charge
Six is a family, seven's too large.

Theme Connections

Babies
Counting
Lullabies
Numbers

You're a Grand Old Flag

You're a grand old flag, you're a high flying flag;
And forever in peace, may you wave;
You're the emblem of the land I love,
The home of the free and the brave.
Every heart beats true 'neath the Red, White and Blue,
Where there's never a boast or brag;
But, should auld acquaintance be forgot,
Keep your eye on the grand old flag.

Theme Connections

Colors
Patriotism

Z

Zoom, Zoom, Zoom

Zoom, zoom, zoom, *(stand, rub hands upwards)*
I'm going to the moon. *(zoom hands up)*
If you want to take a trip,
Climb aboard my rocket ship. *(climb imaginary ladder)*
Zoom, zoom, zoom, *(repeat hand-rubbing)*
I'm going to the moon.

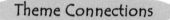

Theme Connections

Outer Space
Sun, Moon, Stars

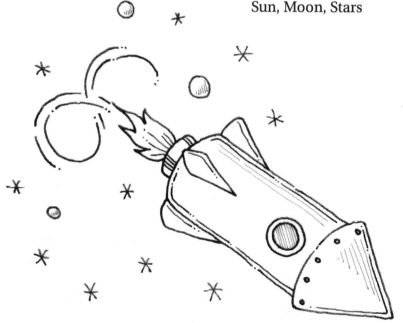

Zum Gali Gali

Zum gali gali gali (*one group sings this chant for whole song)*
Zum gali gali,
Zum gali gali gali,
Zum gali gali

Hechalutz le maan avoda *(another group sings this song)*
Pioneers all work as one
Avoda le maan hechalutz
Work as one all pioneers

Ha shalom le maan ha amin
Peace shall be for all the world
Ha amin le maan ha shalom
All the world shall be for peace.

Theme Connections

Peace
Work

First Line Index

Theme Connections Index

Celebrations

Cleanup

Clothing

Colors

Cowboys/Cowgirls

Days of the Week

Emotions

Families

Farms

Flowers

Food

Insects

Ants

Bees

Butterflies

Caterpillars

Fleas

Months of the Year

Movement

Music

Occupations

Oceans and Seas

Opposites

Outer Space

Parts of the Body

Patriotism

Peace

Pumpkins

Rivers

School

Seasons

Self-esteem

Senses

Shapes

Sounds of Language

Work

Category Index

Call and Response

Chants

Fingerplays

Nursery Rhymes

Rhymes and Poems

Tongue Twisters

Creating Readers

Over 1000 Games, Activities, Tongue Twisters, Fingerplays, Songs, and Stories to Get Children Excited about Reading
Pam Schiller

Instill the basic building blocks of reading with *Creating Readers,* the comprehensive resource that develops a strong foundation for pre-readers. *Creating Readers* gives teachers and parents the tools to teach pre-reading skills with over 1000 games, activities, tongue twisters, fingerplays, songs, and stories for the letters of the alphabet. This invaluable resource develops the child's desire to read as well as the skills needed to begin reading. *Creating Readers* starts children 3 to 8 towards a future rich with books and reading. 448 pages. 2001.

ISBN 0-87659-258-2

The I Can't Sing Book

For Grownups Who Can't Carry a Tune in a Paper Bag But Want to Do Music with Young Children
Jackie Silberg

Who says you need an opera singer's voice to teach music to young children? Fascinating, easy activities help even the most musically-challenged adult bring children the wonder and magic of making and hearing music. All you need are things like rubber bands, paper clips, jingle bells, and paper plates to give the gift of music to children. 174 pages. 1998.

ISBN 0-87659-191-8

gryphon house®, inc.

P.O. Box 207 • Beltsville MD 20704
800-638-0928 • FAX 301-595-0051
EMAIL: info@ghbooks.com
www.gryphonhouse.com

The Complete Daily Curriculum For Early Childhood

Over 1200 Easy Activities to Support Multiple Intelligences and Learning Styles
Pam Schiller and Pat Phipps

Because there's more than one way to be smart! This innovative book for three-to-six-year-olds offers a plan for every learning style. Organized by theme, *The Complete Daily Curriculum for Early Childhood* includes a morning circle and end-of-day reflection, as well as different activities for each learning center. With over 1200 activities and ideas to engage multiple intelligences, plus assessment tools and a comprehensive appendix of songs, stories, games and dances, props, recipes, patterns, chants, rhymes, and arts and crafts, you'll find everything you need to captivate and challenge every child in your classroom. 480 pages. 2002.

ISBN 0-87659-228-0

The Complete Resource Book

An Early Childhood Curriculum
Pam Schiller and Kay Hastings

The Complete Resource Book is an absolute must-have for every teacher. Offering a complete plan for every day of every week of the year, this is an excellent reference book for responding to children's specific interests. Each daily plan contains circle time activities, music and movement activities, suggested childrens books, and six learning center ideas. This book is like having a master teacher at your side, offering you guidance and inspiration all year long. 463 pages. 1998.

ISBN 0-87659-195-0

 gryphon house®, inc.

P.O. Box 207 • Beltsville MD 20704
800-638-0928 • FAX 301-595-0051
EMAIL: info@ghbooks.com
www.gryphonhouse.com

The GIANT Encyclopedia of Circle Time and Group Activities for Children 3 to 6

Over 600 Favorite Circle Time Activities Created by Teachers for Teachers
Edited by Kathy Charner

Open to any page in this book and you will find an activity for circle or group time written by an experienced teacher. Filled with over 600 activities covering 48 themes, this book is jam-packed with ideas that were tested by teachers in the classroom.

510 pages. 1996.

ISBN 0-87659-181-0

The GIANT Encyclopedia of Theme Activities for Children 2 to 5

Over 600 Favorite Activities Created by Teachers for Teachers
Edited by Kathy Charner

This popular potpourri of over 600 classroom-tested activities will engage children's imaginations and provide many months of learning fun. Organized into 48 popular themes, from Dinosaurs to Circuses to Outer Space, these favorites are the result of a nation-wide competition. 511 pages. 1993.

ISBN 0-87659-166-7

gryphon house®, inc.

P.O. Box 207 • Beltsville MD 20704
800-638-0928 • FAX 301-595-0051
EMAIL: info@ghbooks.com
www.gryphonhouse.com

500 Five Minute Games

Quick and Easy Activities for 3-6 Year Olds
Jackie Silberg

Enjoy five minute games that are easy, fun, and developmentally appropriate. Children unwind, communicate, and build self-esteem as they have fun. Each game indicates the particular skill developed. 272 pages. 1995.

ISBN 0-87659-172-1

Transition Tips and Tricks

For Teachers
Jean Feldman

The author of the best-selling book *Transition Time* brings you more attention-grabbing, creative activities to provide children with an outlet for wiggles, while giving their brains a jump start with cross-lateral movement.

Grab their attention with songs, games, fingerplays for any time of the day.

These classroom-tested ideas are sure to become favorites! 216 pages. 2000.

ISBN 0-87659-216-7

gryphon house®, inc.

P.O. Box 207 • Beltsville MD 20704
800-638-0928 • FAX 301-595-0051
EMAIL: info@ghbooks.com
www.gryphonhouse.com